Achieving
QTS

Primary
Science

Teaching Theory and Practice

Achieving QTS

Primary
Science

Teaching Theory and Practice

Third edition

John Sharp
Graham Peacock
Rob Johnsey
Shirley Simon
Robin Smith

LearningMatters

Acknowledgements
Chapter 3: graphs reproduced by Joshua Harris.
Chapter 4: illustrations by Julie Bateman, aged 10.
Chapter 7: class organisation and interactive display diagrams by Joel Morris.
Chapter 8: explanatory pictures reproduced by Joshua, Laura, Jacob and Barnaby Harris. Concept cartoon reproduced from *Concept Cartoons in Science Education* (Naylor and Keogh, 2000) by kind permission of Millgate House Publishers.
Chapter 9: screen shot of circuit diagram from *Interfact: Electricity and Magnetism CDROM* (1997) by kind permission of Two-Can Publishing.
Chapter 10: health and safety diagrams by Joel Morris.

First published in 2000 by Learning Matters Ltd.
Reprinted in 2001.
Second edition published in 2002.
Reprinted in 2002.
Reprinted in 2003 (twice).
Reprinted in 2004.
Reprinted in 2005 (twice).
Third edition published in 2007.

British Library Cataloguing in Publication Data
A CIP record for this book is available from the British Library.

ISBN 978 1 84445 097 8

Cover design by Topics – The Creative Partnership
Text design by Code 5 Design Associates Ltd
Project management by Deer Park Productions
Typeset by PDQ Typesetting Ltd, Newcastle under Lyme
Printed and bound in Great Britain by Bell & Bain Ltd, Glasgow

Learning Matters
33 Southernhay East
Exeter EX1 1NX
Tel: 01392 215560
info@learningmatters.co.uk
www.learningmatters.co.uk

Contents

1
Introduction

About this book

This book has been written to satisfy the needs of all primary trainees on all courses of initial teacher training in England and other parts of the UK where a secure knowledge and understanding of how to teach science is required for the award of Qualified Teacher Status (QTS) or its equivalent. This book will also be found useful by Newly Qualified Teachers (NQTs), mentors, curriculum co-ordinators and other professionals working in education who have identified aspects of their science practice which require attention or who need a single resource to recommend to colleagues.

Features of this book include:

- **clear links with the Professional Standards for QTS;**
- **clear reference to Science in the National Curriculum for children and the QCA/DfES exemplar Scheme of Work for Science at Key Stages 1 and 2;**
- **pedagogical and professional knowledge and understanding for effective science teaching and learning;**
- **research summaries;**
- **practical tasks;**
- **clear links between different aspects of teaching science;**
- **further reading and references;**
- **glossary.**

What is primary science and why is it taught?

Even today, primary science means different things to different people. Considerable and often heated debate in recent years has revolved around the portrayal of primary science as *product*, in which scientific knowledge is arrived at by objective methods capable of yielding accepted concepts, or *process*, in which scientific knowledge is arrived at by subjective acts of individual discovery driven by the development of scientific skills. In terms of the nature, teaching and learning of primary science, both have something to offer and clearly an appropriate balance between the two is required. Primary science is perhaps best regarded, therefore, as an intellectual, practical, creative and social endeavour which seeks to help children to better understand and make sense of the world in which they live. Primary science should involve children in thinking and working in particular ways in the pursuit of reliable knowledge. While practical work undoubtedly contributes towards securing children's interest, curiosity and progress in science, children's scientific knowledge and understanding cannot always be developed through practical work alone. Just as the methods of science need to be taught explicitly, so too does the scientific knowledge and understanding implicit in scientific activities and their outcomes. As Science in the National Curriculum states:

> *Science stimulates and excites children's curiosity about phenomena and events in the world around them. It also satisfies this curiosity with knowledge. Because science links direct practical experience with ideas, it can engage learners at many levels. Scientific method is about developing and evaluating explanations through experimental evidence and modelling. This is a spur to critical and creative thought. Through science, children understand how major scientific ideas contribute to technological change – impacting on industry, business and medicine and improving quality of life. Children recognise the cultural significance of science and trace its world-wide development. They learn to question and discuss science based issues that may affect their own lives, the direction of society and the future of the world.*

Teachers (and trainees) are, of course, instrumental in developing children's scientific ideas and practical abilities and for fostering positive attitudes towards science. Readers wishing to find out more about primary science in general are directed towards the further reading and references sections included at the end of this introduction.

Professional Standards for QTS for Primary Science

Professional Standards for QTS (DfES/TDA, 2006) deals with the subject, pedagogical and professional knowledge and understanding required by trainees to secure children's progress in science. This book refers mostly to the pedagogical and professional requirements (see Johnsey et al., 2007 for subject knowledge and understanding). In summary, by the end of all courses of initial teacher training, all trainees are expected to know and understand:

- the reasons why it is important for all children to learn science and the value of engaging all children's interest in science;
- the nature of scientific understanding;
- key aspects of science underpinning children's progress in acquiring scientific knowledge, understanding and skills and how progress is recognised and encouraged;
- methods of developing children's scientific knowledge, understanding and skills;
- ways of organising and managing science in the classroom;
- assessing and evaluating science teaching and learning;
- the importance of health and safety;
- the benefits of using ICT in science.

You may find it helpful to consult the appropriate sections of the Handbook which accompanies the Professional Standards for QTS for clarification and support.

Science in the National Curriculum

Science in the National Curriculum (DfEE/QCA, 1999) is organised on the basis of four key stages. Key Stage 1 for five to seven year olds (Years 1 and 2) and Key

Stage 2 for seven to eleven year olds (Years 3 to 6) are for primary. The components of each Key Stage include Programmes of Study, which set out the science that children should be taught, Attainment Targets, which set out the science that children should know and be able to do, and Level Descriptions, which outline what children working at a particular level should be able to demonstrate. Science in the National Curriculum is a minimum statutory requirement. Since its introduction in 1989 it has been significantly revised three times. A brief summary of the Programmes of Study is presented as follows:

- **Sc1: Scientific enquiry (Ideas and evidence in science; Investigative skills);**
- **Sc2: Life processes and living things (Life processes; Humans and other animals; Green plants; Variation and classification; Living things in their environment);**
- **Sc3: Materials and their properties (Grouping materials; Changing materials; Separating mixtures of materials – Key Stage 2 only);**
- **Sc4: Physical processes (Electricity; Forces and motion; Light and sound; The Earth and beyond – Key Stage 2 only).**

Science in the National Curriculum also presents some information on the contexts in which primary science should be taught, links to other subjects, technological application, health and safety and the use of ICT.

Science: a Scheme of Work for Key Stages 1 and 2

Use of the exemplar Scheme of Work for Science at Key Stages 1 and 2 (QCA/DfEE, 1998, with amendments 2000) is entirely optional. Designed to help implement Science in the National Curriculum, many schools are, however, beginning to adapt it for their own needs. The Scheme is presented as a series of Units which attempt to provide continuity and progression in primary science provision between Years 1 and 6. Guidance is offered on:

- **the nature and place of each Unit;**
- **how each Unit builds on previous Units;**
- **technical scientific vocabulary;**
- **resources;**
- **expectations;**
- **teaching activities;**
- **teaching outcomes;**
- **health and safety;**
- **ICT links.**

A summary of Units is presented below.

The Teacher's Guide which accompanies the Scheme of Work indicates that, in their long- and medium-term planning, schools may wish to consider alternative sequences of Units. This is, indeed, sound advice!

FURTHER READING   FURTHER READING   **FURTHER READING**

Arthur, J. et al. (2006) *Learning to Teach in the Primary School*. Oxford: Routledge.
Harlen, W. (2001) *The Teaching of Science in Primary Schools*. London: Fulton.

Key Stage 1	
Year 1 Units	**Year 2 Units**
1A Ourselves 1B Growing plants 1C Sorting and using materials 1D Light and dark 1E Pushes and pulls 1F Sound and hearing	2A Health and growth 2B Plants and animals in the local environment 2C Variation 2D Grouping and changing materials 2E Forces and movement 2F Using electricity
Key Stage 2	
Year 3 Units	**Year 4 Units**
3A Teeth and eating 3B Helping plants grow well 3C Characteristics of materials 3D Rocks and soils 3E Magnets and springs 3F Light and shadows	4A Moving and growing 4B Habitats 4C Keeping warm 4D Solids, liquids and how they can be separated 4E Friction 4F Circuits and conductors
Year 5 Units	**Year 6 Units**
5A Keeping healthy 5B Life cycles 5C Gases around us 5D Changing state 5E Earth, Sun and Moon 5F Changing sounds —	6A Interdependence and adaptation 6B Micro-organisms 6C More about dissolvng 6D Reversible and irreversible reactions 6E Forces in action 6F How we see things 6G Changing circuits 5/6H Enquiry in environmental/ technological contexts

Hollins, M. and Whitby, V. (2001) *Progression in Primary Science: a Guide to the Nature and Practice of Science in Key Stages 1 and 2*. London: Fulton.

Millar, R. and Osborne, J. (1998) *Beyond 2000: Science Education for the Future*. London: King's College.

Roden, J. (2005) *Reflective Reader: Primary Science*. Exeter: Learning Matters.

Sherrington, R. (ed.) (1998) *ASE Guide to Primary Science Education*. London: Stanley Thornes.

REFERENCES REFERENCES **REFERENCES** REFERENCES REFERENCES

DfEE/QCA (1999) *Science: the National Curriculum for England*. London: HMSO (*http://www.nc.uk.net*).

DfES/TDA (2006) Professional Standards for Qualified Teacher Status. London: TDA (*http://www.dfes.gov.uk*, *http://www.canteach.gov.uk* and *http://www.tda.gov.uk*).

Peacock, G., Sharp, J., Johnsey, R., and Wright, D. (2007) *Primary Science: Knowledge and Understanding*. Exeter: Learning Matters.

QCA/DfEE (1998, with amendments 2000) *Science: a Scheme of Work for Key Stages 1 and 2*. London: QCA (*http://www.qca.org.uk* and *http://www.standards.dfes.gov.uk/schemes*).

2
The nature of scientific understanding

Introduction

This chapter discusses the very nature of scientific understanding and explores the implications for teaching science in schools. All of us behave in different ways as we learn more about the world around us. Often, however, how and what we learn leads to our own 'personal' understanding rather than that shared and accepted by the scientific community. While not everyone will become a professional scientist, those who use more scientific methods are more likely to have a more realistic understanding of how things are, unlike those who depend on hearsay or make inaccurate observations and poor interpretations.

The nature of science understanding

Science ... is the source of explanations about how and why things happen in the world around us ... [It should be seen] not as a set of facts to be learnt but as a series of explanations which the community of scientists currently considers to be best. (Watt, 1999)

It is easy to see why science has gained the reputation it has in the past. In order to survive an often hostile world, it has been very important to establish how that world behaves and to predict what will happen next. The notion that science can provide watertight explanations and reasons is one we would like to believe in. Unfortunately science cannot always provide clear-cut answers to everything although many would like to believe so. In fact, the methods employed in science, and the body of knowledge which has been accumulated, provide only the best explanations we have so far, based on the evidence gathered and the interpretations put on that evidence.

It is true to say that there is some science that we are very sure about, largely because all the evidence collected over a long time points towards its validity. Thus we are fairly sure that a force due to gravity will always pull an object which is close to the Earth downwards, and plants need a source of light in order to grow healthily. However, a scientist would say that if one day we found evidence that things do not always fall towards the Earth, we should then be prepared to change our views about how gravity works.

The ideas that are commonly accepted by the scientific community form the knowledge and understanding part of any educational curriculum and provide the ideas that scientists use to build new concepts and theories. While we should be ready to consider and reinterpret new evidence, we have to believe in some things or we may never leave our own homes for fear of floating off into outer space! At the same time, however, we must realise (and make others realise, too) that many ideas in science can never actually be proven but they can certainly be falsified.

IN THE CLASSROOM

Some teachers in a primary school noticed that often their children would be noisier and more agitated on windy days. The children came to school across a windy playground where the leaves themselves seemed to be swept up in frenzied excitement. Over a period of time other teachers in the school made the same observation. Some teachers in the school claimed that their own classrooms were always calm despite the weather conditions outside. Observations at playtime on windy days, however, showed that the children from these classes were also particularly excited outside of their own classroom.

Over a period the group of teachers talked to colleagues from other schools and also read articles which supported their ideas about children's behaviour on windy days. The teachers formed a theory concerning the children's behaviour which was supported by keen observation and the collection of a range of evidence. The theory built up over a period of time and in some teachers' minds became fact.

There are a number of points about the nature of scientific understanding which this story can illustrate.

- **The teachers had clarified their ideas about children's behaviour and windy days by making a general statement based on their initial experiences.** *Scientific understanding is based on previously accumulated knowledge which may be expressed in terms of generalisations.*
- **Over a period of time they checked their ideas against new evidence and found them to be consistent with this evidence.** *The more evidence that supports an idea, the more we might accept it as valid.*

- However, even now, they cannot be sure that their ideas provide the best explanation because future observations may disprove them (in which case new, modified ideas may emerge). *Scientific ideas are often tentative*.
- As the teachers made more observations and developed ideas about why the children behaved as they did, a theory emerged which could be tested. As long as the theory was supported by evidence it could be usefully employed by some teachers to predict their children's behaviour and adapt the day's work to suit this. *A successful theory will enable successful predictions to be made.*
- An educational researcher might have been able to take a more scientific approach to testing this theory by making more reliable, consistent and repeated observations. Interpretation of this evidence might have produced a more sophisticated theory which linked weather conditions to the general behaviour of the children, or disproved the theory altogether. *The quality of scientific knowledge and understanding is dependent on the quality of the scientific skills used to gather evidence and interpret it.*

The characteristics of scientific understanding

Harlen (2000, p. 17) describes four characteristics of a modern view of science:

- Science activity is about understanding.
- Science activity is a human endeavour.
- Science ideas are often tentative.
- Science ideas must always be evaluated against what happens in the real world.

Understanding in science involves providing explanations and searching for relationships between events, based on sound evidence. The evidence, however, is gathered and interpreted by human beings who, as we know, don't always get it right. Scientific ideas, then, are not a set of abstract rules set out in a textbook but rather a collection of (in some instances rather shaky) ideas set out by people who have interpreted what they have observed in their own personal way. One scientist may be mistaken or may have made an incorrect interpretation of the evidence. The views of a community of scientists who have critically checked each other's findings is much more reliable.

The tentative nature of all scientific ideas can be illustrated by putting ourselves in the place of those who believed the earth was flat. This view of the world made a great deal of sense to most people who very rarely ventured far from home and could see with their own eyes an approximately flat landscape. This view of the world was acceptable and worked for those people on a day-to-day basis. Only when travellers and explorers confirmed that there was no 'edge' to the world and people began to notice that the masts of ships appeared first over the horizon was this view challenged. The evidence simply did not fit. Nowadays we have even more evidence that the earth is almost spherical in photographs from outer space. If, however, new photographs began to show that the earth was doughnut shaped (unlikely of course), we would have to change our minds on the subject and develop new ideas!

Moral and ethical influences on scientific understanding

There are often more powerful influences on what we believe and perceive of the world besides the interpretation of scientific evidence. Galileo was persecuted by the Church for suggesting a theory which put the Sun at the centre of our solar system with our rather insignificant earth orbiting it. The Church had taught an Earth-centred view of the Universe and felt compelled to suppress the scientific evidence that Galileo produced. Modern debates over scientific developments can be influenced as much by politics and prejudice as by hard scientific evidence. Interpretations of evidence can be purposely or inadvertently misleading as a result of the interpreter's moral or ethical stance. Commercial pressures can encourage unscrupulous groups to misconstrue evidence or even falsify it. In short, scientific progress can be hindered and distorted in a variety of ways.

If children are to cope in a modern technological society they must come to appreciate the ways in which scientific knowledge is generated and the ways in which scientific ideas have been developed as a result of human endeavour. While a science curriculum will define a body of knowledge that is apparently fixed and irrefutable, teachers must issue a warning that this is not necessarily so. This can often be achieved through a discussion of the tentative nature of the children's findings in their own investigations. The children themselves know just how shaky some of their experimental results are and should understand that all scientists will have suffered the same kind of problems.

Science and design and technology

Sometimes it is important to know what science is not, in order to understand what it is. To many people, science and technology are spoken of in the same breath as though they were one thing but this is to misunderstand an important fact. Science is to do with finding out about how the world around us works and how it behaves. This is achieved through formulating and testing theories and models by collecting and interpreting evidence. The purpose is to generate reliable knowledge. Design and technology, on the other hand, is primarily concerned with solving problems and satisfying human needs. It draws heavily on the knowledge gained in science and other disciplines, but it uses this knowledge to achieve a different end.

A science curriculum needs examples of technology to help children further understand the science. Children need to understand the implications of using science ideas. When debates rage over such things as genetically modified crops or the use of nuclear power stations, the argument is with the technologists – those who are employing the knowledge gained through scientific pursuits. The pure scientists only supply the knowledge they have gained.

Device knowledge

Research by McCormick (1999) into the way children carry out design and technology tasks focused on the way in which the children applied their knowledge in a practical problem-solving situation. He found that while children might be working on a product with a number of scientific features, their discussions about it were not made in an abstract scientific language. He describes how two children were designing and making a collecting box in which a coin made a model bird move. Their discussions involved a technological language which was closely related to the actual model rather than the scientific or mathematical language they might have employed in a formal science lesson.

McCormick concluded that the information needed in the practical context was subtly different to that gained in the more theoretical science lesson. He called this knowledge 'device knowledge'. This suggests something about the nature of science knowledge as taught in schools and points towards a need for greater links to be made between this type of knowledge and the device knowledge often used in the practical world.

Implications for science teaching

The science curriculum should provide young people with an understanding of some key ideas-about-science, that is, ideas about the ways in which reliable knowledge of the natural world has been and is being obtained. (Millar and Osborne, 1998, Recommendation 6)

The National Curriculum for science in primary schools appears to be set out largely in terms of science facts and concepts (Sc2, 3 and 4). These are the 'big' science ideas about which we are fairly certain and which are deemed appropriate for primary-age children to understand. It is right that teachers teach these ideas as firmly held concepts but this should be done alongside stories about the some-times tentative nature of modern science and about how some old ideas have been modified or replaced throughout history. At the same time teachers will want to teach the skills described in Sc1 – Science enquiry – to illustrate the way in which scientific ideas have been arrived at in the past and are arrived at today.

A SUMMARY OF **KEY POINTS**

> **Science is about understanding the world around us – technology is about using this knowledge to solve problems.**

> **Scientific understanding is based on accumulating and interpreting evidence for proposed theories or models.**

> **Science ideas are often tentative but the 'big ideas' are well established.**

> **Science is a result of human endeavour and thus scientific interpretations may be influenced by moral, ethical, political and commercial factors.**

Moving on

During your Induction year you will be expected to develop *a secure knowledge and understanding of the subject areas you teach* (Professional Standards for

Teachers, I 15). Use the Further Reading section which follows to discover what others believe about the nature of science.

FURTHER READING   FURTHER READING   FURTHER READING

Driver, R., Leach, J., Millar, R. and Scott, P. (1996) *Young People's Images of Science.* Buckingham: Open University Press. This book provides an insight into the nature of scientific understanding as a whole as well as how children's ideas about the nature of scientific understanding develop.

Ollerenshaw, C. and Ritchie, R. (1997) *Primary Science – Making it Work*. London: Fulton. This book provides a general introduction to teaching primary science, drawing heavily on the constructivist approach – one which has been adopted particularly by the science education community.

Peacock, G. A. (2002) *Teaching Science in Primary Schools*. London: Letts. A clear but brief introduction to the intricacies of teaching science in the primary school.

REFERENCES REFERENCES **REFERENCES** REFERENCES REFERENCES

Harlen, W. (2000) *Teaching, Learning and Assessing Science 5–12*, 3rd edn. London: Paul Chapman.

McCormick, R. (1999) 'Capability lost and found', *Journal of Design and Technology Education*, 4(1), 5–14.

Millar, R. and Osborne, J. (1998) *Beyond 2000 – Science Education for the Future*. London: King's College.

Watt, D. (1999) 'Science: learning to explain how the world works', in J. Riley and R. Prentice (eds), *The Curriculum for 7–11 year olds*. London: Paul Chapman.

3
Processes and methods of scientific enquiry

Introduction

IN THE CLASSROOM

A class of six- and seven-year-olds were working in the small garden the school had created. The tasks for the day were planting and weeding but several children had become fascinated by the small creatures they found as they worked. One group looked under stones and discovered more. Some children had names for creatures they saw. Others pointed out how they moved. Their teacher had not planned for this to be the focus of the science but it fitted the school scheme of work well, since they were studying the variety of life and conditions for living things. She recognised its potential to develop scientific enquiry from the children's curiosity and interest. Before they went any further she talked with them about being careful not to harm any creatures. Some children wanted to make homes for the ones they had found. The teacher asked what they thought these would have to be like in order to start them thinking about the types of environment which different animals needed. She anticipated helping them investigate the conditions which the small animals preferred, working with them to devise simple tests of light/dark, damp/dry.

The class had already been shown how to use a magnifying glass and viewers, so they would be able to make closer observations to check the claims they were making about how many legs each creature had. The teacher thought that drawing and maybe modelling might improve the observations. That would also help them compare different animals with pictures in books and she could introduce simple keys and some software the school had. Grouping pictures, sorting activities and games might help children get an idea of a simple classification. At present some of them were using terms like worm and insect but there were lots of disagreements over what to call each new find. The teacher could see opportunities for language work in these debates, and there would be maths to apply in drawing charts or graphs if they found lots of things. She could also see some challenges in organising all this – not least with the two children who didn't want to have anything to do with 'creepy-crawlies'.

This scenario illustrates some opportunities to develop processes and methods used in scientific enquiry, not all of which are exclusive to science. Compare it with the way that the National Curriculum 2000 describes what children should do at this stage.

During Key Stage 1 pupils observe, explore and ask questions about living things, materials and phenomena. They begin to work together to collect evidence to help them answer questions and to link this to simple scientific ideas. They evaluate evidence and consider whether tests or comparisons are fair. They use reference materials to find out more about scientific ideas. They share their ideas and communicate them in language, drawing, charts and tables. (p. 78)

When they build on this during Key Stage 2 one sign of progress is that children carry out more scientific investigations.

Investigations and other sorts of practical work

Investigations are an important part of science in primary schools. They develop children's understanding of scientific procedures and concepts, their knowledge and their skills.

Investigations are not simply practical work. Practical activities may be used for various reasons, for instance to illustrate a scientific concept, to teach a specific skill or to foster observation. These are all worthwhile. However, it is important to be clear about the purpose of any activity – for example, giving children a detailed set of instructions to follow so they reach a predetermined result may be appropriate if we are aiming to teach skills or to reinforce ideas. But this is not the same as children carrying out investigations where the aim is to allow them to use and to develop concepts, skills and procedural understanding. When they are investigating, children have some responsibility for deciding what to do and how to do it. They should be encouraged to think for themselves, to use their knowledge and skills, and to extend their understanding.

Characteristic features of investigations

Children may have to work out exactly what question they are trying to answer and turn it into a form that can be investigated.

They use investigative procedures, such as:

- **raising questions;**
- **identifying and controlling variables;**
- **planning;**
- **observing/measuring;**
- **analysing data;**
- **interpreting results;**
- **deciding how far their findings answer their original question;**
- **evaluating their work.**

A whole investigation may include all these features. However, we often support children by organising investigations so that they can concentrate on a few aspects. We also have to teach them the skills and knowledge that they need in order to carry out investigations. Although children are taking responsibility for their investigation, teachers have an active part to play – they are not simply providing hands-on experiences nor adopting a discovery approach to science learning.

PRACTICAL TASK PRACTICAL TASK **PRACTICAL TASK** PRACTICAL TASK

Consider a common practical activity in primary science – bouncing balls.

1. How might you organise the activity if you want to teach a skill – e.g. careful measurement?

2. How might you organise the activity if you want to ensure all the children get a good set of results that can be used to see patterns in results and a relationship between the height of drop and height bounced?

3. How might you organise the activity if you want to extend children's skills at planning a fair test where the key variables are tested and others are controlled?

4. How might you organise the activity if you want children to carry out an investigation of their own?

Make notes or draft a lesson plan for each of these different objectives.

Now we have an overall picture of investigations we will look at some of the features in more detail.

Raising and framing questions

Children ask lots of questions although, sadly, many are discouraged even before they arrive at school. So teachers may have to encourage them to raise questions through devices such as unusual displays, boxes or boards where children can post questions. When starting new topics lists of potential questions can be brainstormed and used in planning the work with the children. There should be a school climate where questions are treated seriously and teachers should be role models. They will certainly need to help children pose questions that are framed so that they can investigate them and find something out. That is a crucial step in any research. The skill can be scaffolded with class discussion to refine questions posed by the children or teacher, with support for small groups working on their own ideas, through direct suggestions and through active redrafting of written questions. As they gain experience and confidence children can be challenged more:

- **Are they making use of what they already know to pose their question and predict what might happen?**
- **Have they thought about different ways their question could be investigated?**
- **What skills have they learned already that would help them with the investigation?**

Fair testing and other kinds of investigations

Primary teachers have been very active in teaching children about the need for fair tests. These are investigations in which the key independent and dependent variables are systematically changed and measured while the others are controlled so they do not change. The independent variable is the one that will be changed intentionally to see what effect it has on the dependent variable which will be measured. Variables are those things which change or vary in an investigation.

How do children and teachers know what they are likely to be in any specific case, for example when testing materials to see which is most effective for keeping someone warm? Well, their previous experiences of clothing and the scientific knowledge they have about materials will suggest some factors. The level of their understanding about how heat travels can make a difference to what factors they see as relevant. Children may need lots of help to work out which variable they are going to control, i.e. keep the same, and which they will change. By trying out their ideas practically they may find other things which affect the results. Teachers need a good understanding themselves of the skills and ideas that the tasks may demand – for instance, being able to use a thermometer, knowing the difference between heat and temperature. They have to be aware of practical difficulties and safety issues – can the water be hot enough for the children to get good results? And they also need to be alert to what the children are thinking – for example, do they expect water to go on cooling to zero rather than room temperature? Do they interpret 'fair' as meaning everybody has a go?

In many investigations, variables can be difficult to control or they may interact. Some people also argue that fair tests have been emphasised too much to the detriment of other valuable work.

RESEARCH SUMMARY RESEARCH SUMMARY **RESEARCH SUMMARY**

Watson et al. (1998) pointed out that many investigations do not fit the model of fair testing. They proposed a classification of types of investigation with the aim of encouraging a more balanced approach. They summarised their article as follows:

> The dominance of 'fair testing' in school science investigations is challenged. The inherent characteristics of different kinds of investigations are described. Six different kinds of investigations are: classifying and identifying; fair testing; pattern seeking; exploring; investigating models; and making things or developing systems. A typical set of investigations is analysed, highlighting the dominance of fair-testing investigations and the under-emphasis of other important kinds of investigations.

In their survey half of the investigations teachers reported at Key Stage 2 were of the fair test kind. Another finding was that a few familiar activities accounted for a large proportion of these. Other studies confirm this and also show how children may repeat the same investigation several times during their schooling.

This is not an argument against teaching children how to carry out controlled tests, but rather one for giving them experience of other kinds of investigation and other contexts. This range of work is not easy to fit in when teachers feel that the time available for primary children to do extended science investigations has been squeezed by the National Curriculum, literacy and numeracy hours. So it is crucial to avoid repetition. This is true both within and across key stages.

Planning investigations

In order to plan their own investigations, children need to be able to think ahead, anticipating what they will do and what equipment they will need, how they will record their findings and what they will do with the results. This is demanding and they will need a lot of help. In the early stages teachers will do most of the planning for the children but should aim to involve them and make them aware of the process. Even young children can be given responsibility for planning part of an investigation. In their play they imagine and organise their activities. As they colla-borate in groups and extend their communication skills children become able to take on more of the planning themselves. For teachers in primary schools nowa-days there is a tension between fostering this independence and following the prescribed curriculum.

When they have had some experience of science activities children can do more systematic planning of their investigations. Many teachers have found planning sheets helpful to structure this and to support children. These can be provided through a computer, on paper or on a larger-scale board. A few key headings or questions direct children's attention to things they should think about before they start. For instance, for a 'fair test' kind of investigation.

- **What are we trying to find out?**
- **What are we changing?**
- **What do we want to keep the same?**
- **What do we think will happen?**
- **What are we going to measure?**
- **How will we record our measurements?**
- **What equipment do we need to collect before we start?**

The headings should prompt children to think through the stages of an investiga-tion one at a time. They can help them focus their attention, be organised and think ahead to consider alternatives or problems. They might be referred to as a remin-der during their investigation. The structure can also reinforce children's understanding of the procedures involved in an investigation. However, we should beware that such aids do not become straitjackets. Planning sheets usually emphasise one sort of investigation, the fair test. They may also become a routine or even a ritual, taking time and attention away from the investigation itself.

So we need to be clear about our purpose for requiring the children to plan – and to share the purpose with them.

- **Is it so they are more likely to do an appropriate investigation for the question they posed?**
- **Because they might miss important observations?**
- **So they think about the variables that need to be controlled?**
- **Because they have to plan what measurements to take and get the equipment?**
- **Is our aim to increase their understanding of the scientific procedures in a whole investigation?**

REFLECTIVE TASK

Science investigations can also serve a broader purpose across the curriculum: fostering children's creativity and their thinking skills.

Recall investigations you have done yourself or with children.

1. What can a teacher do in order to encourage pupils to generate lots of possible ways of investigating a question? What might inhibit children from thinking of alternative ideas?
2. How can pupils be helped to decide on the most appropriate ways?
3. How confident would you be at letting pupils follow up their own ideas even if they looked like being unsuccessful? How do you decide whether to intervene?

For further ideas look at the points cited from Summerfield (1997) in the Research Summary near the end of this chapter.

Observation and measurement

Careful observation is an important skill to develop in science. Teachers can use devices such as viewing frames or magnifying glasses to help children look more closely. They can ask children to report on changes over time, for example when food colouring is dropped into water. Audiotapes and videotapes can be replayed so they can check their observations. Teachers' questions can be used to focus or extend children's observations as appropriate: sometimes it is best to draw their attention to relevant features and at other times to ask them what else they notice.

The questions and problems that lead to investigations are often the result of observations, especially of noticing surprising features or unusual events. Observing is not simply looking or listening but is a deliberate act influenced by our expectations and experience. As children gain more scientific knowledge they can be asked to use that to inform their observations. In investigations they should be drawing upon their scientific ideas from the start. Observation features at later stages as well. Some kinds of investigation depend on lots of carefully recorded observations to see if there are any patterns, for example if they want to investigate food preferences of birds visiting a school bird table. Children have to be prepared to make these – they may have to get equipment, practise using it, and decide when to make and how to record their observations. Some investigations combine qualitative records and measurement, for instance if they trace the germination and growth of plants under various conditions or keep a record of the weather.

Measuring is a key feature of science, although not all scientific work by children will involve measurement. Children need to see the purpose for measuring in their investigations. They should be helped to think about what they are going to measure and how they can do so. If they are going to need to use measuring instruments do they already know how to? Have they been taught how to use them appropriately? Are they seeking to be accurate and are they aware of errors? Consider, for instance, children carrying out a very common activity, rolling vehicles they have made down slopes to see which runs fastest. Children often opt to time these using a digital watch or stopclock and report their results. However, the error in switching the clock on and off can be considerable, and they need to realise this and to consider what else they might measure.

In tests like this children are often expected to make repeated measurements. This is good practice but once again we have to be careful that they learn to do it with understanding.

RESEARCH SUMMARY RESEARCH SUMMARY **RESEARCH SUMMARY**

Varelas (1997) worked closely with eight groups of nine to ten year olds exploring the relationship between the height of a ramp and the distance a toy car travelled when rolled down it. She watched, asked questions and videotaped the lessons. These children had an integrated maths and science curriculum which taught them to make three measurements in investigations and then find the average by taking the middle number, the median. Although each group did this, she found they did not understand the procedure in the way that scientists would. Most of them expected to get different measurements each time but they held differing views about the value of doing multiple trials. A few showed some awareness of how errors could affect results. Some suggested they would get nearer to the 'true value' as they did more, others felt that fewer trials were better. Their conversations as they worked out which number to use when they had done their trials were revealing. One group decided they didn't really know why they were repeating the tests so 'why don't we only do one trial, so we scratch off all the other ones and leave the first one?' Another group felt that three or five trials would work but not ten because 'there's no middle number in 10'. Three children did not think one number could represent their trials so they would report the range or all the measurements. Those who did use one number to represent their trials had various ways of selecting it.

Some of the equipment they will use during investigations may be met first in maths when they measure time, length, weight and volume. As they progress through simple comparison, use of non-standard measurements to standard measures they acquire skills that they can use in science. They are also learning about accuracy and choice of the appropriate scale. Other equipment such as spring balances to measure forces or thermometers may be introduced in science lessons. They will need to be taught how to use these with skill and understanding, for example beginning with learning to read a simple scale on sturdy thermometers, progressing to recognising the range they can measure using more sensitive instruments, handling them carefully, and reducing errors by waiting for the liquid to reach a steady reading and viewing them correctly. At level 3 they are expected to be able to use a range of simple equipment to measure quantities like mass and length; by level 5 they should be selecting apparatus, planning how to use it, making a series of measurements with appropriate precision, and beginning to repeat measurements.

ICT (Information and Communication Technology) has brought new aids such as dataloggers with sensors that children can use to make and record measurements (see p. 99). These devices and software can help them handle the data they produce, see patterns and relationships and communicate it. The links between the maths, science and ICT curricula are most obvious in the area of data handling.

Handling data: recording and interpreting results

Young children need lots of help to organise their data collection and recording. The simplest form of recording is to present results directly, for instance by making a display that shows plants grown in different conditions or by placing materials in order from strongest to weakest as they are tested. Children at all stages can use tape recorders, digital cameras or video recorders to capture observations; this could be especially useful to enable children with communication problems to focus on the science and achieve their potential.

Progression in this aspect of their work can be illustrated by reference to the National Curriculum levels. At level 1 children will be using pictures and simple charts. If drawn large they can be displayed and discussed as the first step in interpreting data. Talk and writing are important for communicating findings at any stage and mathematics contributes other ways of presenting results that children need to apply. In the early stages teachers may provide a simple tally chart or table but as they progress children should begin to plan their own. At level 2 they are expected to use simple tables where appropriate. If they are to progress teachers need not only to introduce them to other ways of recording but also to help them see patterns in data that have been recorded. At level 3 they are expected to record their own observations in a variety of ways and to provide explanations for simple patterns in recorded measurements. To build on that they need to learn about using different sorts of tables, begin to plot points in simple graphs and use these graphs to interpret patterns in their data. At level 5 children should be able to make decisions about the best way to record and present particular sorts of data. Software such as spreadsheets and databases may assist them to process lots of data and to try different ways of displaying it – tables, bar graphs, pictograms, line graphs, scattergrams. But we should ensure they are taught to use them with understanding. For example, they should realise when there is a relationship between variables that makes it appropriate to draw a line graph but also when that is not appropriate

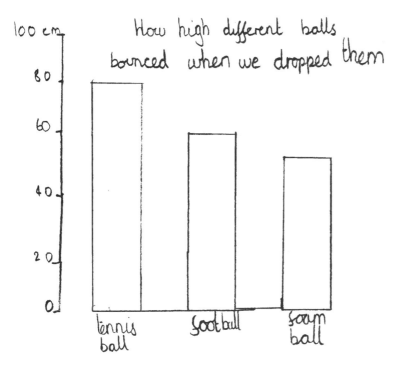

Figure 3.1 Bar graph

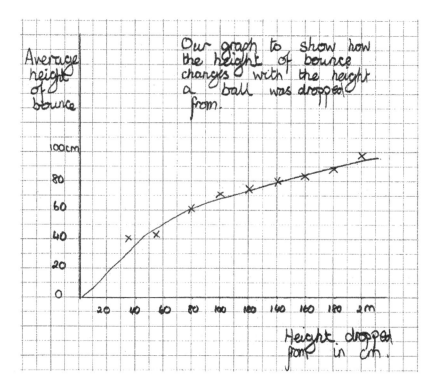

Figure 3.2 Line graph

Children can work at different levels on related investigations in one class, as in these examples of bouncing balls. Those who drew the first graph were working at a lower level in science and in maths. The teacher had suggested they compare how high different balls bounced. They chose the balls and did the tests without a lot of help but they only made one measurement for each, using a metre rule. This sort of graph was familiar to them. The second graph was drawn by the most able children in the class who practised first in order to measure the height of bounce as accurately as possible. Then they fixed a scale on the wall, dropped the ball at 10 cm intervals, made three readings for each and took the median value. They realised that a line graph could be drawn to show the relationship between the two heights. In a previous investigation of cooling they had plotted points for temperatures and had learnt to draw a line of best fit. When they drew this one they decided after discussion that they could take the line back to zero, even though when they had dropped the ball from less than 40 cm they had not got reliable measurements.

As well as acquiring these skills and the procedural understanding to apply them, children at level 5 and above should be using their data to draw conclusions which are based on evidence and which relate to scientific ideas. This is the purpose of doing whole investigations. But the skills to enable this sometimes have to be taught separately and then put together. In some ways interpreting results is the hardest of these. It requires the child to scrutinise data for patterns, to relate the findings to their predictions yet be open to unexpected results, and to draw on scientific ideas while their understanding is limited. There is plenty that teachers can do to help children with this as they progress through the primary school.

- Talk about patterns and regularities in everyday events, for example daily cycles or shadow lengths.
- Draw attention to phenomena which indicate relationships, for example how seedlings grow towards a window or how many snails are about on wet days.
- Display children's work so that patterns are apparent and discuss them, for example the shadows cast by a puppet figure at different distances from a lamp or the order in which parachutes of different sizes fell. Include questions in displays.
- Ask them to refer back to their predictions when they discuss the results of a test they did.
- Organise activities where measurement reveals relationships, for example between pulse rates and exercise.
- Provide tables or graphs with results for children to analyse and discuss, for example elastic bands stretched by loading masses. Introduce some with less tidy sets of results and ask for their explanations, for example the distance travelled by cotton reels powered by turns of elastic band or the readings on a spring balance pulling increasing loads.
- When they report their findings ask children to provide explanations and suggest reasons if any of their results do not fit the pattern.
- Encourage them to give reasons based on their science studies when they predict and offer explanations.
- Establish a climate where children challenge one another's explanations and offer alternative interpretations and listen to one another.

Evaluating

Evaluating is valuable for improving investigations and developing procedural understanding. However, it should not become a ritual or a chore. Nor do we want children to feel defensive about their work. Specific, focused questions will be more helpful at first rather than general enquiries about how they could make it better. For example, if children were recording something changing over time, ask how they decided when to take measurements, whether any measurements needed to be checked, what was difficult, what worked well. As children become more capable at planning investigations they can look back at their plan to see how closely they followed it, what adjustments they had to make as they went and how they would advise another group to tackle the same question. If several groups investigate similar questions they can compare their findings and discuss why they may not have the same results. The time available for repeating and refining investigations is limited so we need to make the best use of any opportunities. Much of the evaluation can occur as children talk about the work they are doing. We also have to bear in mind that children often find science stimulating because they are actively engaged in practical work and trying out their own ideas. Teachers need to listen and watch them at work in order to judge whether a question will extend the children's understanding or be seen as a distraction. Let us end this chapter by illustrating some ways in which teachers successfully develop their children's thinking as they investigate.

RESEARCH SUMMARY RESEARCH SUMMARY **RESEARCH SUMMARY**

John Summerfield (1997) observed three teachers organising investigations with their Key Stage 2 classes. Among the features he saw that contributed to successful learning were:

- **the explicit creation of an enthusiastic climate of enquiry where children knew that their ideas, questions and interpretations really mattered;**
- **managing time and resources so that children could follow up ideas;**
- **questioning and teaching that fostered investigative independence.**

Three types of question which seemed especially effective were those which:

1. reviewed children's own grasp of science concepts being drawn upon in an investigation;
2. encouraged speculation and a willingness to seek evidence;
3. prompted children to explain what they might do next or what they had found out.

Prompt questions were sometimes asked in order to 'nudge forward investigative action and reflection by pupils'. When one eight year old who was testing absorbency of papers said, 'It took ten seconds to get that much', pointing to the soaking paper, his teacher replied: 'So how will you know which one has soaked up the most water, and in what order?' The dialogue that followed prompted him and his group to evaluate what they had done and then to improve their investigation.

A SUMMARY OF **KEY POINTS**

> **Practical activities may be used for various reasons: to investigate a question or problem; to illustrate a scientific concept; to teach a specific skill; to foster observation.**

> **Investigations are an important part of science in primary schools. They develop children's understanding of scientific procedures and concepts, their knowledge and their skills.**

> **When they are investigating, children should be encouraged to think for themselves, to use their knowledge and skills, and to extend their understanding.**

> **Children should be taught to use and to understand investigative procedures such as: framing a question in a form that can be investigated; identifying and controlling variables; planning; observing; measuring; analysing data; interpreting results; deciding how far their findings answer their original question; evaluating their work.**

> **Science investigations can be stimulating, enjoyable and challenging for children – and for their teachers!**

Moving on

As you become more familiar with children in your class during your Induction year you will be able to plan to assess individual needs and abilities in the context of investigations. This information should be used to set individual targets and assist pupils to reflect on their own learning.

FURTHER READING   FURTHER READING   FURTHER READING

Among the many useful publications for primary teachers that are produced by the ASE (Association for Science Education) several are specifically about investigations.

The AKSIS project (the ASE and King's College Science Investigations in Schools) has focused on Key Stages 2 and 3. Their first publication was *Getting to Grips with Graphs – From Bar Charts to Line of Best Fit*. They have produced a resource pack bringing together the evidence from their research with a wealth of helpful guidance and ideas.

Brown, A., Campione, J., Metz, K. and Ash, D. (1997) 'The development of science learning abilities in children', in K. Harnqvuist and A. Burgen (eds), *Growing up with Science: Developing Early Understanding of Science*. London and Bristol, PA: Jessica Kingsley and Academia Europaea, pp. 7–40. A useful chapter if you want to read recent evidence about how children learn and how far they can think in scientific ways. The later chapters contain reviews of topics such as concepts in the curriculum, progression, gender and evaluation by authorities from the UK, Europe and the USA.

Goldsworthy, A. and Feasey, R. (1997) *Making Sense of Primary Science Investigations*, 2nd edn. Hatfield: ASE. This is an earlier book from the ASE which teachers have found really useful. It contains lots of examples that illustrate well progression in each aspect of investigations.

Goldsworthy, A. et al. (2000) *Investigations: Developing Understanding in Scientific Enquiry.* Hatfield: ASE.

Smith, R. G. and Peacock, G. (1995) *Investigations and Progression in Primary Science*. London: Hodder & Stoughton. The first part of this book explains the main features of investigations and how they can be taught. The second part illustrates how 12 familiar themes can be investigated appropriately at three different levels. It contains suggestions for teaching children to make progress in the classroom and planning for whole school progression, with examples of how to set tasks and ask questions.

REFERENCES   REFERENCES   REFERENCES   REFERENCES   REFERENCES

Summerfield, J. (1997) 'Inside the investigative classroom: what's going on?', *Primary Science Review*, 46, 4–7.

Varelas, M. (1997) 'Third and fourth graders' conceptions of repeated trials and best representatives in science experiments', *Journal of Research in Science Teaching*, 34(90), 853–72.

Watson, R., Goldsworthy, A. and Wood-Robinson, V. (1998) 'What is not fair with investigations?', *School Science Review*, 80(292), 101–6.

4
Children's ideas

Introduction

Children begin to learn science from their earliest interactions with the world around them. Their everyday experiences enable them to develop ideas and explanations about what they see, feel and do. Yet to fully appreciate and understand their world, children need to have a system for organising their ideas and testing out their explanations. Learning science can help children to make sense of natural phenomena, by introducing organising 'concepts', and by providing a range of 'contexts' in which children can explore their ideas and test their explanations. Through learning science children can also build on and extend their everyday experiences in such a way as to provide them with interest and intellectual stimulation. This chapter examines children's ideas, focusing in particular on the ways in which these ideas have implications for teaching and learning science.

Children's learning

To understand how children learn science, and the importance of children's ideas in the learning process, teachers need to have some knowledge of the nature of children's learning. Much has been written on this topic and is beyond the scope of this chapter, but a useful introduction to how children think and learn is provided by David Wood, as shown in the following Research Summary.

RESEARCH SUMMARY RESEARCH SUMMARY **RESEARCH SUMMARY**

In his book *How Children Think and Learn* (1998), Wood documents the changes that have taken place over several decades in theories about children's learning. He provides a synthesis of the theories of three influential thinkers: Piaget, Bruner and Vygotsky. Wood shares with Piaget the view that children actively 'construct' their knowledge of the world. He points out that Piaget's theory, with its emphasis on the active, constructive nature of human development, is often referred to as a 'constructivist' approach. Wood also summarises the ideas of Bruner, who, while accepting the image of children as active in the construction of their own understanding, also stressed the role of social interaction on human development. In addition, Wood provides a useful account of the theory of Vygotsky, who emphasised the role of communication, social interaction and instruction in determining the path of development. Approaches which focus on the importance of social interaction are referred to as 'social constructivism'. Wood (p. 17) acknowledges the importance of social interaction in the development of children's ideas:

> Social interactions (particularly those which take place between children themselves) may facilitate the course of development by exposing a child to other points of view and to conflicting ideas which may encourage him to re-think or review his ideas.

Many developments in science education in the last 20 years have been influenced by constructivist and social constructivist theories of learning. In essence, a constructivist view of learning suggests that learning involves an active process in which each learner is engaged in constructing meanings, whether from physical experiences, dialogue or texts. A constructivist perspective has underpinned many studies into children's ideas undertaken in different parts of the world. Highly influential projects include the New Zealand Learning in Science Project (LISP), the Children's Learning in Science Project (CLISP) and the primary Science

Process and Concepts Exploration (SPACE) project. The following Research Summary provides an overview of some of this work.

RESEARCH SUMMARY RESEARCH SUMMARY **RESEARCH SUMMARY**

Osborne and Freyberg (1985) report findings from a range of studies from the LIS Project which show that from a young age, prior to any teaching and learning of formal science, children develop meanings for many words used in science teaching, and views of the world which relate to ideas taught in science. The findings also show that children's ideas are strongly held and are often significantly different to the views of scientists, and that these ideas are sensible and coherent views from the children's point of view, often remaining uninfluenced or influenced in unanticipated ways by science teaching.

Though concerned with the teaching of science in the eleven to fourteen age range, the research carried out by Driver and her colleagues as part of the CLIS Project has been influential in the practice of science teaching at both secondary and primary level. Driver's early work (Driver, 1983) focuses on the need for teachers to recognise and act upon children's ideas, particularly those ideas that differ from accepted scientific ideas which are referred to as 'preconceptions' or 'alternative frameworks'. Reviews of the wide range of research into children's ideas in different parts of the world can be found in Driver et al. (1985) and Driver et al. (1994). These texts provide useful insights for teachers at all levels. Driver's subsequent research explored children's ideas about the nature of science (Driver et al., 1996).

The SPACE project set out to discover the ideas primary school children have about science and to consider ways of helping children to develop a more scientific understanding. The SPACE team produced a wide range of research reports, each focusing on a different topic in science (for example, Watt and Russell, 1990; Osborne et al., 1991). In addition, individual members of the project team have produced books and contributed chapters to various other works (Harlen, 1993, 2000; Osborne, 1995; Black, Osborne and Simon, 1997; Wadsworth, 1997; Watt, 1998; Harlen and Qualter, 2004). The project also led to the publication of the widely acclaimed Nuffield Primary Science curriculum materials.

The research into children's ideas has shown several features which will now be considered separately in order to emphasise their importance in the teaching and learning of science. The way in which children's ideas can be addressed in teaching is referred to in later sections, which include reference to constructivist teaching approaches.

Children's ideas can be very different

Children's ideas are personal constructs which are formed from their experience and the interactions they have with other children and adults. Though children often develop similar ideas about natural phenomena, and there is evidence to show that some ideas are common to children in different parts of the world, they do have different life experiences which influence the way their ideas develop. During a study carried out into children's understanding of forces, a sample of 12 children aged between eight and ten were asked individually what they could tell the teacher about gravity. Even in this small sample of children there was a range of different ideas:

'Gravity is something to do with space.'
'Gravity keeps you up.'
'Gravity is in the air.'
'There is no gravity in space or water because you can float.'
'Gravity in space makes you float around.'
'Gravity is not acting on birds or flying things.'
'Gravity stops things floating.'
'Gravity makes you come down.'
'Gravity keeps you on the ground.'
'Gravity pulls things down.'
'Gravity is a force pulling things down.'
'Gravity pulls all objects down.'

Without further discussion with the children it is difficult to tell what they mean by short statements such as these.

The SPACE publications previously cited describe ways of categorising children's ideas, which are usefully summarised by Wadsworth:

- *Anthropomorphic views*. For example, 'I think the little caterpillar is scrunched up in that little egg waiting to hatch, but while she is waiting she's planning her life.'
- *Egocentric views*. For example, 'We've got to go to bed. We can't sleep when it is light.'
- *Ideas based on a colloquial use of language*. For example, some children believed that you need to eat carrots to see at night. Everyday language carries an implicit concept that vision is an active process, for example 'cast our gaze', 'stare daggers'.
- *Ideas based on limited experience and observations*. For example, some children represent the body as a hollow cavity filled to the neck with blood, because when we cut ourselves, blood comes out.
- *Stylised representations*. For example, children may draw the sun with lines radiating out from it, but this does not mean that they understand that light travels in straight lines.

The SPACE project also found that some children expressed ideas which are more closely related to scientific views than those shown above.

The idiosyncrasy of children's ideas reflects their individual life experiences; it is only to be expected that children's limited experiences result in ideas which differ from the accepted scientific view. From the categories of ideas described by Wadsworth it can be seen that many children's ideas are very far from the scientific view. A common idea, also prevalent among adults, is that plants obtain 'food' from the soil; the use of the word food is confusing, as plants do obtain nutrients from the soil. What is difficult for children to understand is that plant material is generated mainly from carbon dioxide and water. Incomplete understanding of scientific ideas sometimes prevents children from making distinctions between separate scientific ideas; when children see a solid substance turning into a liquid, for example ice melting, or sugar crystals dissolving, they often believe that similar processes are in operation.

Write down your own explanation of the distinction between melting and dissolving. Consider your explanation and identify what children need to know and understand in order to engage with your explanation.

A further feature of children's ideas is that they can be very specific to particular contexts. A study exploring children's understanding of balanced forces demonstrated the way in which children's explanations of the same underlying principle can be different in different contexts. In the study children were presented with two different situations involving balanced forces, a box suspended from a piece of elastic and a box supported on a bendy bridge. Children were often inconsistent in the way they identified downward and upward forces acting on the box, though the same principle applied in each case (the upward force of the distorted material balancing the downward force of gravity). Children tend to see different situations as instances of different phenomena, so much so that they may switch from one explanation to a contradictory one.

RESEARCH SUMMARY RESEARCH SUMMARY **RESEARCH SUMMARY**

Sylvester Bradley (1996) provides a good example of how nine-year-old Joy drew two completely contradictory ideas about how she was able to see a candle and a cup. The drawings looked like this:

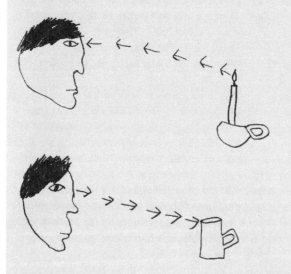

(Adapted from Sylvester Bradley, 1996)

Joy realised that the candle emitted light, and that the light travelled from the candle and entered her eye. However, she was not aware that objects also scatter light. She thought that as the cup obviously did not emit light, her eye must be actively sending out light instead and so she drew the light travelling from her eye to the cup. Holding two different models of vision presented no problem to Joy, as she focused only on aspects of the situation that she could see.

In summary, children have different ideas according to their limited experiences. Yet children's ideas make logical sense in terms of these experiences, which often means that these ideas are hard to change.

Children's ideas are hard to change

Because children's ideas make personal sense, they can be very stable and resistant to change. Even when presented with evidence to show that their ideas are not sufficient to explain phenomena, children may ignore the evidence, or interpret it in terms of their own ideas. The following Research Summary demonstrates an example of a child's ideas which were resistant to the teacher's attempts to change them; the extract also raises questions about the strategies a teacher might use to effectively challenge children's ideas, which will be referred to in a later section.

RESEARCH SUMMARY RESEARCH SUMMARY **RESEARCH SUMMARY**

Sylvester Bradley (1996) describes the case of a six-year-old child, Lynsey:

Lynsey, aged six, held an extremely stable idea about the digestive system, which her teacher could not persuade her to change.

First we chew the food up. Then there are two tubes, one for food and one for drink. Then some muscles mush it together. Then it comes out of one end.

Lynsey knew from her own experience that solid and liquid foods go separately into the body. She also knew that solids and liquids are eliminated separately from the body. She thus concluded that they must pass through the body separately, and so the idea of two distinct tubes made complete sense to her. Lynsey was not prepared to change her idea at that particular time, despite being shown pictures of the digestive system. She was adamant that her digestive system was not the same as those in the pictures.

More recent work on this topic can be found in an interesting article by Teixeira (2000).

Children – and indeed many adults – find that many scientific ideas are counterintuitive, in that they seem contrary to everyday experience. A typical example that is difficult for many people to understand is that heavy objects fall through the air at the same rate as lighter objects unless the lighter objects are slowed by air resistance. Because so many objects, like feathers, are slowed by air resistance, people's experience tells them that heavy objects, like hammers, must fall more quickly.

REFLECTIVE TASK

Think of an idea that you have had which you found hard to change to a more scientific view. Write down your idea and an explanation for why you found it so resistant. In a small group compare and discuss the difficulties that you and your colleagues experienced.

Having described some of the features of children's ideas in this and the previous section, the following sections focus on ways in which children's ideas can be elicited and their misconceptions addressed during teaching.

Eliciting children's ideas and recognising children's misconceptions

When considering children's ideas it is important to understand the distinction between partial understandings and those ideas which are misconceived. Children construct ideas which make sense to them personally, on the basis of their life experiences. Looking back at the ideas children expressed about gravity, one can see why children believe that gravity does not act on birds as they fly – because the birds are not pulled down to earth. Yet how does a child come to say that gravity keeps you up? With ideas such as gravity, which include specialised scientific terms, one can perhaps assume that children have misinterpreted what they have heard, or have been given insufficient opportunity to establish the accepted scientific meaning. Other ideas, like Lynsey's idea about her digestive system, have been constructed on the basis of experience and are hard to change because they involve structures which cannot be seen directly. It is important to be aware that children's ideas form in different ways, from their exposure to language and meaning and from their limited experiences. In helping children to develop a more scientific understanding of any particular idea, teachers need to find ways of recognising children's misconceptions and challenging them.

There are various methods that can be used for finding out about children's ideas which have been adopted in research and are used in teaching. The SPACE project used informal classroom techniques for eliciting children's ideas. The techniques included the following:

- *Using log-books* – children could make drawings or do writing over a period of time, to provide a record of long-term changes.
- *Structured writing or drawing* – children could write or draw responses to particular questions from the teacher. Sometimes drawings could be annotated to clarify explanations.
- *Completing a picture* – children could be asked to add relevant points to a picture.
- *Individual discussion* – teachers could ask open questions and listen to children talking about their ideas.

These techniques can be used in the classroom for exploring children's ideas in a range of science topics. In addition, the SPACE team used exploratory activities to find out about children's ideas. For example, in the topic of electricity, children were provided with simple electrical materials, i.e. light bulbs, wires and batteries,

Figure 4.1 A child's drawing of a bulb and battery (adapted from Osborne et al., 1991, p. 31)

and then asked to draw the connections that would be needed to light a bulb on a pre-drawn diagram of a bulb and battery. The drawing illustrates an example from a nine-year-old child.

PRACTICAL TASK PRACTICAL TASK PRACTICAL TASK PRACTICAL TASK

The SPACE team concluded that this drawing reflects an understanding which sees the battery as a source of power, the light as the consumer and the wire as a necessary link to enable the supply. Discuss this interpretation with a colleague. How might you be sure the child has this understanding?

Finding out about children's ideas requires a learning environment in which children feel free to express their views. Some children require more confidence that others to contribute their ideas, particularly if they feel that the teacher wants the 'right answer'. Work undertaken by Keogh and Naylor over many years has addressed this issue. Their highly successful concept cartoons were designed to help children talk about 'other' children's ideas. More recently, Keogh and Naylor have launched a major initiative to use large puppets to enhance children's engagement and talk in science. Research into the use of puppets has shown these to be a useful teaching strategy for eliciting children's ideas.

RESEARCH SUMMARY RESEARCH SUMMARY RESEARCH SUMMARY

Research and development into the use of concept cartoons (Naylor and Keogh, 2000) has shown these to be highly successful devices for eliciting children's ideas in science. Building on this success, Keogh et al. (2006) undertook research into the use of puppets to promote engagement and talk in science. In this project primary teachers used large hand-held puppets to create characters that would express alternative ideas, so that children would more readily respond and express their own ideas. The research has shown that children are not only keen to tell the puppet what they know, but also listen more attentively when the puppets are used. Children are more motivated to ask or answer questions and join in discussion.

Analysis of classroom talk before and after using puppets has shown that children are found to use more reasoning when they talk in response to the puppets, justifying their ideas about scientific concepts. Moreover, puppets have been shown to engage children who are usually reluctant to contribute. Puppets have now been used successfully across the range of 4–11 years.

The research with puppets has helped to confirm the recent emphasis on the importance of talk and social constructivist ideas in primary education. A useful booklet by Alexander (2004) discusses the issue of talk in UK primary schools, where he raises the question:

> *Do we provide and promote the right kind of talk; and how can we strengthen its power to help children think and learn more effectively than they do?*

The theme of different kinds of talk in science classrooms is also usefully discussed by Asoko and Scott (2006), and by Mercer et al. (2004) in their research, which has shown that children using 'exploratory talk' are able to achieve a better understanding of science.

A constructivist teaching approach

Once children's ideas have been elicited and the teacher has recognised their misconceptions and partial understandings, decisions need to be made about how to challenge these ideas and help children to develop a more scientific understanding. Such decisions are central to teaching approaches based on a constructivist view of learning. To teach constructively, the teacher aims to adopt strategies which challenge children's existing ideas and enable children to construct new knowledge for themselves. Though the research studies cited previously have all been influenced by a constructivist perspective, there are different theories about the ways in which children change their ideas. Harlen proposes a model of learning which places an emphasis on the importance of process-skills such as hypothesising, predicting and interpreting in changing children's ideas; in its discussion of students' ideas about particles the CLISP team focuses on the need for children to distinguish the difference between observation and theory, and emphasises the importance of theoretical models in developing children's scientific understanding. Reference to these studies is required for a more extensive discussion about how children construct scientific knowledge and understanding.

As part of their research programme, the SPACE team developed intervention strategies for helping teachers to address children's misconceptions and partial understandings.

RESEARCH SUMMARY RESEARCH SUMMARY RESEARCH SUMMARY

The SPACE research reports include accounts of how teaching interventions were planned to challenge children's ideas and help them to construct a more scientific understanding. Good summary accounts of two of these interventions are provided by Watt (1998) as a case study of teaching about sound, and Black et al. (1997) on the topic of light, taken from Osborne et al. (1991). For example, to help children understand the idea that light travels in straight lines, they were given the problem: 'How could they make the light go round every side of the table?' A strong torch, mirrors and plasticene were provided and the children had to discuss a preliminary solution before attempting the activity. The drawings they produced were used for discussion with the teacher.

Watt (1998) lists the techniques developed in the SPACE project which characterise a constructivist teaching approach. These include:

- **building on children's ideas through investigation, posing questions for children to consider and providing opportunities to test ideas;**
- **testing the 'right' idea alongside the children's ideas;**
- **making imperceptible changes perceptible, for example using evidence such as videos of time-lapse photography of plant growth;**
- **helping children to generalise from one specific context to others;**
- **refining children's use of vocabulary.**

Watt points out that these techniques relate to Harlen and Osborne's (1985) primary constructivist approach, in which the teacher is a facilitator, valuing children's ideas and providing support and appropriate opportunities for scientific investigation. A more recent collection of accounts of teaching primary science constructively is provided by Skamp (2004).

REFLECTIVE TASK

Refer back to Lynsey's idea about her digestive system. Discuss with a colleague different ways in which Lynsey's teacher could help her to change her ideas.

In order to extend their understanding of science concepts, it is useful to teach children that ideas which apply in one context may also apply to different subject matter. For example the same principle lies behind the evaporation of water in sweating, drying paint, puddles drying up and the water cycle. Analogies can also be used to help make complex scientific principles more comprehensible. The following classroom story provides an example of a teacher using an analogy to help children understand that light enters the eye through the pupil.

IN THE CLASSROOM
Fiona and the little black dot

Fiona asked the children to draw how they see a book. She then asked the children to think about their drawings and to tell the whole class how they thought they see things. Some children said 'eyes' and 'light', which Fiona acknowledged, then one child said 'you need that little black dot in front of your eye'. Fiona asked the children if they knew what this black dot was called. One child gave 'pupil', so Fiona then asked the children if they knew what the pupil was. They could not answer this other than suggest 'to make you see', so Fiona used this idea of the pupil to provide the children with a useful analogy which would help them to understand how light enters the eye. She said:

It's actually a hole. If you imagine your eyeballs are ping pong balls? You've got a hole in the front and a cover on it so things don't get in, what you can see there is actually a hole. How many of you have been to the doctor's or been to see a nurse and they've looked into your eyes? The thing is they are actually looking inside the hole at the back of your eyeball.' (Adapted from Osborne and Simon, 1996)

Though analogies are useful, they can have limitations and children may take them too far. A commonly used analogy when teaching about electric current is that the current is like water flowing around a circuit. However, if the circuit is broken, electric current does not leak out in a puddle, as water would. The same caution applies to the use of physical models, though these are essential in science teaching. Models are used to represent phenomena which are too large, too small or difficult or impossible to see; a globe can be used to represent the Earth; marbles can be used to show the arrangement of particles in solids, liquids and gases; a model torso can show the organs of the body. When concrete models are used teachers need to point out their limitations.

Working from children's ideas can be challenging. Once a teacher has elicited children's ideas, decisions have to be made about how to respond to and value these ideas. Also, there are management decisions about how to group children for the purpose of testing out their ideas. Should children with the same ideas be grouped, or is it better for children with different ideas to work together? It may be that disagreement between children enables them to develop their ideas further. There are other issues to be considered relating to the status of knowledge in the classroom. For example, making children's ideas the centre of attention by asking for and accepting them may serve to reinforce them. In addition, a constructivist approach may not result in children reaching a more scientific view, in which case the children may be in the process of guessing the right answer in order to produce it in a test. Teachers need clear objectives for learning within a constructivist approach, and strategies for differentiation which enable children to learn through appropriate discussion and activity.

A SUMMARY OF **KEY POINTS**

Children's ideas:

> **are constructs which are formed from their experience and social interactions;**

> **can be very different due to children's individual experiences;**

> **make logical sense in terms of these experiences;**

> **are strongly held and can be resistant to change;**

> **are often significantly different from the accepted views of scientists.**

A constructivist approach to teaching emphasises:

> **elicitation of children's ideas;**

> **identification of misconceptions and partial understandings;**

> **testing out children's ideas and alternative ideas through investigation.**

Moving on

As you move into your induction year you will have opportunities to explore your pupils' ideas in more detail. You will begin to perceive patterns and commonly held beliefs about the physical world and to experiment with approaches which challenge children's ideas.

FURTHER READING   FURTHER READING   FURTHER READING

Harlen, W. (2000) *Teaching and Learning and Assessing Science 5–12*. London: Paul Chapman Publishing. This is the third edition of Harlen's comprehensive view of many issues discussed in this chapter.

Skamp, K. (ed.) (2004) *Teaching Primary Science Constructively*, 2nd edn. London: Harcourt Brace. A collection of articles focusing on ways in which different science topics can be taught using a constructivist approach.

SPACE research reports, for example:

Osborne, J., Black, P., Smith, M. and Meadows, J. (1991) *Primary SPACE Project Research Report: Electricity*. Liverpool: Liverpool University Press.

Watt, D. and Russell, T. (1990) *Primary SPACE Project Research Report: Sound*. Liverpool: Liverpool University Press.

Each report provides useful insights into children's ideas and intervention strategies used to address misconceptions.

Watt, D. (1998) 'Children's learning of science concepts', in R. Sherrington (ed.), *ASE Guide to Primary Science Education*. Hatfield: Association for Science Education. A useful case study of the SPACE research and discussion of the issues of teaching science using a constructivist approach.

REFERENCES REFERENCES **REFERENCES** REFERENCES REFERENCES

Alexander, R. (2004) *Towards Dialogic Teaching: Rethinking Classroom Talk*. York: Dialogos.

Asoko, H. and Scott, P. (2006) 'Talk in science classrooms', in W. Harlen (ed.), *ASE Guide to Primary Science Education*. Hatfield: Association for Science Education.

Black, P., Osborne, J. and Simon, S. (1997) 'Concepts in the primary science curriculum', in K. Harnqvist and A. Burgen (eds), *Growing Up with Science*. London: Jessica Kingsley.

Driver, R. (1983) *The Pupil as Scientist?* Buckingham: Open University Press.

Driver, R., Guesne, E. and Tiberghien, A. (1985) *Children's Ideas in Science*. Buckingham: Open University Press.

Driver, R., Leach, J., Millar, R. and Scott, P. (1996) *Young People's Images of Science*. Buckingham: Open University Press.

Driver, R., Squires, A., Rushworth, P. and Wood-Robinson, V. (1994) *Making Sense of Secondary Science: Research into Children's Ideas*. London: Routledge.

Harlen, W. (1993) *Teaching and Learning Primary Science*. London: Paul Chapman.

Harlen, W. (2000) *Teaching and Learning and Assessing Science 5–12*. London: Paul Chapman Publishing.

Harlen, W. and Osborne, R. (1985) 'A model for learning and teaching applied to primary science', *Journal of Curriculum Studies*, 2(17), 133–46.

Harlen, W. and Qualter, A. (2004) *The Teaching of Science in Primary* Schools, 4th edn. London: David Fulton.

Keogh, B., Naylor, S., Downing, B., Maloney, J. and Simon, S. (2006) 'PUPPETS bringing stories to life in science', *Primary Science Review*, 92, 26–8.

Mercer, N., Dawes, L., Wegerif, R. and Sams, C. (2004) 'Reasoning as a scientist: ways of helping children to use language to learn science', *British Educational Research Journal*, 30(3), 359–77.

Naylor, S. and Keogh, B. (2000) *Concept Cartoons in Science Education*. Millgate House Publishers.

Osborne, J., Black, P., Smith, M. and Meadows, J. (1991) *Primary SPACE Project Research Report: Electricity*. Liverpool: Liverpool University Press.

Osborne, J. (1995) 'Science from a child's perspective', in S. Atkinson and M. Fleer (eds), *Science with Reason*. London: Hodder & Stoughton.

Osborne, R. and Freyberg, P. (1985) *Learning in Science*. Auckland: Heinemann Educational.

Osborne, J. and Simon, S. (1996) 'Primary science: past and future directions', *Studies in Science Education*, 26, 99–147.

Sylvester Bradley, L. (1996) *Children Learning Science*. Oxford: Nash Pollock Publishing.

Teixeira, F. M. (2000) 'What happens to the food we eat? Children's conceptions of the structure and function of the digestive system', *International Journal of Science Education*, 22(5), 507–20.

Wadsworth, P. (1997) 'Document 9: Children's ideas in science', in P. Murphy (ed.), *Making Sense of Science Study Guide*. Buckingham: SPE/Open University.

Watt, D. (1998) 'Children's learning of science concepts', in R. Sherrington (ed.), *ASE Guide to Primary Science Education*. Hatfield: Association for Science Education.

Watt, D. and Russell, T. (1990) *Primary SPACE Project Research report: Sound*. Liverpool: Liverpool University Press.

Wood, D. (1998) *How Children Think and Learn*. Oxford: Blackwell.

5
Teaching strategies

Professional Standards for QTS

Those awarded QTS must have a secure knowledge and understanding of science that enables them to teach effectively across the age and ability for which they are trained. To be able to do this in the context of the nature of scientific understanding trainees should:

Professional attributes

Q1 Have high expectations of children and young people including a commitment to ensuring that they can achieve their full educational potential and to establishing fair, respectful, trusting, supportive and constructive relationships with them.

Q2 Demonstrate the positive values, attitudes and behaviour they expect from children and young people.

Professional knowledge and understanding

Q10 Have a knowledge and understanding of a range of teaching, learning and behaviour management strategies and know how to use and adapt them, including how to personalise learning and provide opportunities for all learners to achieve their potential.

Q14 Have a secure knowledge and understanding of their subjects/curriculum areas and related pedagogy to enable them to teach effectively across the age and ability range for which they are trained.

Professional skills

Q22 Plan for progression across the age and ability range for which they are trained, designing effective learning sequences within lessons and across series of lessons and demonstrating secure subject/curriculum knowledge.

Q25 Teach lessons and sequences of lessons across the age and ability range for which they are trained in which they:

(a) use a range of teaching strategies and resources, including e-learning, taking practical account of diversity and promoting equality and inclusion;

(b) build on prior knowledge, develop concepts and processes, enable learners to apply new knowledge, understanding and skills, and meet learning objectives;

(c) adapt their language to suit the learners they teach, introducing new ideas and concepts clearly, and using explanations, questions, discussions and plenaries effectively;

(d) manage the learning of individuals, groups and whole classes, modifying their teaching to suit the stage of the lesson.

Introduction

Teaching science in the primary school can be exciting and stimulating for both teachers and children. Children respond well to the practical, exploratory nature of the subject, especially if the topics of science are related to their everyday lives. As with all subjects, teachers need to vary their approach so that children feel that each lesson holds something new. This chapter describes a variety of strategies that teachers might adopt in order to provide a range of learning activities in primary science.

There are a number of principles to bear in mind when choosing the most appropriate strategy to suit individual circumstances. These are discussed first.

Guiding principles for choosing appropriate strategies for teaching science

- **Whatever happens in the classroom, children should become better and better at thinking and behaving scientifically and understanding scientific ideas.**

It is possible for the majority of children in a classroom to be happily carrying out science activities for an hour or so but to have learnt nothing new by the end. Teachers need to use their knowledge of the children, based on previous assessments, to plan work which takes them another step on. The work should be challenging, stimulating and demanding. Children should be motivated to learn rather than merely occupied by the experiences provided.

When it comes to developing children's procedural skills, these need to be practised in a meaningful context which provides a new challenge at the same time as reinforcing skills already acquired.

- **Teachers should gain some insight into the ideas that children hold in a science topic before extending this knowledge.**

The National Curriculum for primary science is apparently written in such a way that assumes all children in a class will have reached a certain level of understanding by a certain time and will all be ready to move on to the next stage together. Research has shown this not to be the case and that children learn by restructuring the ideas that they currently hold only when new information is sufficiently plausible and intelligible. The elicitation of children's ideas before a science topic begins enables the teacher to plan work which is more appropriate for groups of children.

See page 26, Chapter 4

- **Teachers should provide a range of experiences which will lay the foundations for helping children understand the big science ideas later in life.**

Primary teachers need not think that they should always be able to explain why things are so to children. Often it is more appropriate to enable children to experience and observe a certain phenomenon without necessarily understanding all aspects of it. If teachers, then, have an idea where these experiences are leading, they will be able to lay suitable foundations for future learning. For instance, children might observe and record the similarities and differences between some liquids and solids so that one day they will be able to understand the particulate nature of all matter. The knowledge of where the children are heading will influence the kind of questions the primary teacher might ask.

- **Practical activities should be used when appropriate but there are instances when alternative strategies should be used.**

Children who learn about what is inside the human body or about the solar system are unlikely to do this completely through practical activities. Secondary sources of information such as pictures, video or the use of models are more likely to be used as well as analogy. Often a profitable combination of practical activity, together with other strategies such as reading, drawing or discussion, will achieve the teacher's objectives.

- **Teachers should be clear about which skills and concepts they want children to learn and bring these to the fore in any lesson.**

Children do not soak up skills and knowledge simply by being exposed to a scientific idea through activity. It is important that teachers teach the key ideas directly though asking appropriate questions and directing the child's attention towards the significant parts of a concept.

- **Teachers should use language precisely in science so as not to cause confusion. It should be recognised that the language used can contribute to the organisation of understanding in science.**

Our everyday use of such words as *force* and *plant food* often give rise to misunderstandings in science. Teachers need to be aware of the potential for such confusion and to provide with care good examples of scientific language. The use of the correct linguistic 'labels' can enable children to organise their thoughts on a subject and to convey their understanding to the teacher.

- **Whenever possible exploit the links between science and other areas of the curriculum.**

Cross-curricular links can provide meaningful contexts for science, making what appears to be a rather abstract concept more relevant to the children's lives. At the same time the application of scientific ideas in new contexts, such as a design and technology lesson or history lesson, will help to reinforce these ideas. Furthermore, cross-curricular work will enable the teacher to assess children's understanding of science concepts in new contexts.

Teaching strategies

Teachers gain a wide repertoire of approaches and strategies for delivering the curriculum throughout their careers. Varying the approach to teaching is crucial to motivating children to learn and to a teacher's own professional development. The remainder of this chapter looks at a range of strategies which might be employed to teach science in the primary classroom.

Starting with children's ideas

Good teaching in primary science involves understanding the ideas that children hold on a topic and then planning work which enables them to challenge and reconstruct their ideas. There are a variety of strategies that teachers can use to elicit children's ideas. These include:

These are described on page 30, Chapter 4

- observing children investigating;

- discussion with children (individuals, groups, whole class);

See page 89, Chapter 8

- concept mapping;

- structured writing or making annotated drawings;

See page 87

- creating a poster;

- using a floor book to record ideas in a group;

- discussion cartoons;

See page 83

- completing a picture or drawing a comic strip to explain a phenomenon;

- giving a short written test.

See page 85

Teacher exposition

Teacher exposition and explanation has an important part to play in the effective teaching of science. This will often happen more during the introductory or plenary phases of a lesson when the teacher has the attention of the whole class, but of course it may take place while the children work individually or in groups.

Teachers might adopt some of the following strategies when explaining science.

- Recap on the children's previous learning in the same science area.
- Focus on the important aspects of the science idea and avoid introducing irrelevant or confusing material.
- Where appropriate, use models, analogies or illustrations to support the teacher's explanation.
- Use a physical demonstration to accompany an explanation if appropriate.
- Use a picture or an artefact to base discussion around.
- Pass things round for the children to handle if possible.
- Simplify the science concept so that communication is at the child's level.
- Break down the science idea into smaller, easily understood parts.
- Backtrack and simplify an idea if the children clearly do not understand the first explanation.
- Use question and answer to ascertain the children's general knowledge and understanding.
- Relate the science idea to an event that is familiar to the children.
- Keep teacher explanations short and to the point (alternatively a *discussion* may be a prolonged affair).
- Accompany the explanation with a true story if this is appropriate.
- Weave the explanation into a fictitious story if this seems appropriate.

Teacher demonstration

A physical demonstration may be used as part of a teacher's exposition. This is often easily controlled with the children sitting, listening, watching and participating. Teacher demonstration to the whole class should be used where appropriate and should never take the place of child activity where this is possible. There are a number of points to bear in mind when demonstrating science ideas to children.

- **Ensure that all the children can see what you are doing. Try to demonstrate with large pieces of equipment.**
- **Consider moving your position around the classroom as you demonstrate.**
- **Make the demonstration short and snappy. (The children will be itching to have a go too.)**
- **Involve the children with practical tasks and questions.**
- **Reinforce the main points of the demonstration by following up with a simple child activity or perhaps some form of recording of ideas.**
- **If possible, arrange for small groups of children to gain, after the demonstration, first-hand experience of the equipment you have used.**

IN THE CLASSROOM

Mrs Smith wanted to demonstrate to her Year 2 class of children how the human skeleton enables the body to move through the use of muscles and joints. She had arranged to borrow a large, full-size, plastic skeleton and had it hanging in the classroom as the children came in from playtime. The children assembled on the carpet as the skeleton loomed above them.

Mrs Smith focused on two key ideas in her demonstration: (a) the fact that joints are necessary between sets of bones in order for movement to take place, and (b) the way in which a muscle acts on a bone to pull it into place. All the children were asked to feel the bones in their own bodies as they looked at them on the model and some were asked to pin the names of some of the bones on the model.

Movement of parts of the body was demonstrated by Mrs Smith and some of the children. The skeleton was made to scratch its head and kick a football (how many bones had to move?). A large elastic band was fixed to the forearm to demonstrate how a muscle might pull it upwards and another showed how another muscle would pull it back.

The demonstration was followed by an activity in which the children made a working model of an arm with elastic bands for the biceps and triceps muscles while small groups of children took a closer look at the model skeleton itself.

Using practical activities in primary science

Practical activity in science means that children have some kind of hands-on experience, often involving one or more of the senses. For instance, children may be sorting and classifying a collection, making measurements, or arranging equipment for an investigation.

Primary children enjoy learning through practical activity. They will often claim that 'we haven't been doing any work today' when most of their work has been of a practical nature. This is probably a sad reflection on the fact that most school work is centred on 'sitting and writing' and that practical activity is a novelty for many children. Science teaching in the primary school lends itself to practical activity so teachers should take advantage of this fact.

Practical work can be planned and organised in different ways. Teachers need to be aware of the variety of approaches which are possible and that there are times when alternative teaching strategies will be more appropriate. Medium-term science planning should ensure a balance of practical work and other ways of learning.

Practical work might include:

- **a guided illustrative activity to teach a concept;**
- **an investigative activity including planning and carrying out scientific enquiry;**
- **the observation of a particular phenomenon;**
- **an activity to develop a particular scientific skill (including the use of equipment).**

These four categories of practical work are not exclusive. For instance, observation activities may form part of a broader science investigation. An example of this might be when children need to learn how to use a stopwatch as part of an activity which illustrates how pulse rate changes with exercise.

Here are further examples of these types of practical activity.

- **An activity in which children learn that higher pitched notes are made by shorter stretched elastic bands. (*Illustrative activity*)**
- **Children make a full size model of a daffodil to learn about the parts of a flower as well as to enhance their observational skills. (*Observation activity*)**
- **Children planning and carrying out an experiment to find which materials are best at blocking sounds from reaching the ear. (*Scientific enquiry*)**
- **A short activity in which children 'play' with a collection of magnets to see what they will do. (*Observation activity*)**
- **Children making drawings of a snail as it moves over a leaf. (*Observation activity*)**
- **Children measuring the force required to move things such as an open door, or a work tray or to lift a wooden block. (*Skills activity*)**
- **A problem-solving activity in which children design the best parachute in order to learn more about air resistance and the effects of gravity. (*Involves all categories!*)**

Organising practical work in science
Teachers need special skills in order to organise practical work for their children. They will need to answer the following questions.

- **Should all children in the class do the same practical work at the same time?**
- **Should all groups do the same practical work at the same time?**
- **What sort of groups should the children work in – individual, friendship groups, ability or attainment groups, etc.?**
- **How will the equipment be distributed, shared, maintained and collected in?**
- **How much space is needed for the practical work? Does the furniture need rearranging?**

See page 67, Chapter 7, for a consideration of child grouping and organising resources and time

- **How much of the lesson should be spent on the practical aspect?**
- **What will the teacher's role be during the practical work?**

Teachers will not stop teaching once their introduction is finished and the children are busily employed. Often they will take the role of facilitator or consultant as they sort out the problems of missing equipment, misunderstood instructions, social grouping, and so on. A much more important role is achieved through the use of questions and explanations which provoke thought, provide new ideas and assess learning. The teacher will want to talk to the children and stand back and observe their actions and thoughts when appropriate rather than spend every minute troubleshooting. This can be achieved through thorough planning and organisation and by encouraging the children to become independent learners.

Another important function of the teacher during a practical science lesson is to maintain pace. The teacher will gain a sense of when to stop an activity to draw together some important point and when to allow the children to continue with their individual work. Having a short discussion about one group's achievements so far will often point others in the right direction and send messages about how the teacher wants the whole class to behave.

- **Which key points will be learnt during an activity and which key questions will promote learning?**

See page 60 for more on asking questions

The answer to this question lies within the teacher's own subject and pedagogical knowledge and understanding of science. The teacher must know where the children have come from and where they are going with the particular science being taught. The key ideas are spelt out in the learning objectives for the lesson and should be small enough to be digested by most children in the class. It should be made clear to the children what they are expected to learn from an activity, rather than leaving this to chance. The preparation of some key questions to ask in the introduction, development or conclusion of the lesson will help.

In The Classroom

Mrs Jones's learning objective for her lesson on pushes and pulls with her Year 1 class was written as follows:

> At the end of the lesson most children will have identified three different ways of describing movement – getting faster, getting slower and keeping the same speed.

The children were given a range of cartoon pictures showing moving objects such as toy cars and model swings. The children worked together to reproduce what was in the pictures with cars and swings which had been arranged on the table. They were encouraged to talk about the ways they moved.

Mrs Jones prepared some key questions/challenges for the lesson which she shared with her classroom assistant and parent helper:

- Is the toy car moving?
- Can you make it move faster?
- Is the toy car moving fastest at the top of the slope or at the bottom?
- Can you describe how the movement of the swing is changing?

• **How will the children be given instructions during an activity?**

Teachers will need to consider a range of strategies for giving instructions to children as they carry out practical activities. The obvious strategy of explaining what to do in the introduction to the lesson can have its limitations as many teachers have found. Different ways of conveying instructions are as follows.

1. Using regular verbal instructions as the activity proceeds. This, however, assumes the children will all be working at the same pace.
2. Writing instructions on the blackboard/whiteboard/poster.
3. Using a commercially produced workcard.
4. Using a teacher-designed or commercially available worksheet. The worksheet might be used:
   – as a list of instructions for carrying out science activity;
   – as a comic strip sequence to explain what to do;
   – to write observation records on;
   – to write answers to questions on;
   – to complete a table/picture/graph, etc.;
   – as a planning proforma;
   – as an information text.
5. Briefing a classroom assistant who is assigned to a particular group.

• **How will the children consolidate their learning during or after an activity? What kind of written records should be expected?**

Children might summarise or consolidate what they have learnt from a practical activity in a variety of ways. A discussion of the main points of the lesson, led by the teacher, is a useful way to conclude a lesson. Sometimes groups or individuals can be called upon to describe what they have done and learnt. Children might use a variety of recording methods in which they reflect upon what they have been doing. A group poster or a wordprocessed report are just two examples.

See page 59 for more on concluding a lesson

• **What sort of behaviour should be expected during an activity?**

Teachers will devise their own set of rules for appropriate behaviour in practical science lessons. They will need to decide if it is appropriate for children to talk to others in their group or in the room as a whole. The nature of practical work, often involving cooperation with others, will almost certainly require group or partner discussions but general noise levels may need to be controlled. Teachers must decide if free movement around the room is safe and/or desirable.

See page 74 for more on behaviour

Secondary sources of information

There are some instances where primary school children may not learn by first-hand experience. Science activities may often involve them in reading or working at a computer station. Books, videos and CD-ROMs, as well as listening to and watching their teacher, provide children with secondary sources of information. Teachers should plan to integrate these secondary sources of information within lessons to provide a balance of learning experiences and learning styles. Secondary sources of information are particularly useful where the science would otherwise be inaccessible or dangerous to undertake, where children's knowledge and understanding can be enhanced and extended appropriately, or simply where they provide the most effective way of teaching.

Quite often a child can consolidate learning from a secondary source by carrying out a practical activity.

In The Classroom

Julie and Sarah had used a CD-ROM to discover that the Earth was just one of nine planets which orbit the Sun and that the Moon orbits the Earth. Their teacher encouraged them to make a working model of the Earth-Sun-Moon System so that they could fully understand how each body moved in relation to the others.

The girls completed their own card model which enabled the Earth to rotate around a paper fastener and the Moon to orbit the Earth on a disc of card. They were able to use this model to proudly show their teacher how night and day occurred. After some thought-provoking questions from their teacher they were surprised to learn that the Moon could be present in the sky during day time as well as at night and wanted to know from their teacher why they could not usually see it during the day.

Teachers will want to ensure their children get a balance of practical and other experiences in science, with one strategy being used to complement the other.

Use of role-play

Role-play in which children act out certain scenarios can provide a useful alternative teaching strategy when appropriate. Teachers might use this strategy to promote debate about science ideas such as the misrepresentation of scientific data or to explore contemporary scientific issues. In contrast, children can be encouraged to imagine they are part of a food chain or perhaps an electron in an electrical circuit and explore the science concepts involved in this way.

In The Classroom

Miss Appleton's Year 6 class were involved in the 'How we see things' Unit from the QCA/DfEE Scheme of Work for Science. She wanted them to further explore the idea of reflection by using role-play. In a physical education lesson she had them working in pairs to demonstrate the actions of a reflection in a mirror. The children had observed that a right hand raised produced a corresponding movement in the left hand of the image in the mirror. Now they were able to use this information in their role-play. At the same time they were able to simulate the information they had gained about the distance of the subject and image from the mirror.

Back in the classroom an interesting discussion developed about the relationship between an actor, a mirror and the camera. Was it true that an actress had to look at the camera when she looked in a mirror on screen, and if so, how was she able to put on make-up and comb her hair 'on camera'?

Presentations and debate

Children might work in groups or as individuals to prepare and present a variety of science ideas. This might include the results and conclusions of an experiment, their ideas on how shadows are formed, or their predictions as to which food their collection of snails will prefer. Children can use a variety of multimedia devices to enhance their presentation. Posters, a blackboard or an overhead projector might be employed as well as a computer screen.

Debates or discussions about the moral and ethical dimension of science have a value in promoting both scientific literacy and an appreciation of a wide range of issues.

Use of ICT to support learning in science

Information and communications technology can be used in a wide range of ways to support science learning. This classroom tool provides just one more strategy to be used in order to vary the way in which children learn science.

See page 96, Chapter 9

Teachers' questions

One of the most effective strategies for teaching primary science is for teachers to use a wide range of questions to prompt thoughtful responses in their pupils. Questions can be classified as open-ended or closed types but not all questions fit neatly into these categories. Questioning is a skill which is learnt with practice and experience since it often involves 'thinking on one's feet'.

See page 60, Chapter 6

Teachers use open and closed questioning for a variety of reasons.

- **To elicit children's ideas**
  Can you tell me how you think the bulb lights up?
  How can you hear the sound made by the guitar string?
- **To help make connections between new and existing knowledge**
  Now that you have seen the bread dry up on the window sill how is this like the saucer of milk which we saw dry up the other day?
- **To highlight the steps in a causal sequence**
  What has happened so that the condensation forms on the glass of cold water?
- **For discussion, prediction and explanation**
  How do you think the flat piece of paper will fall?
  Why do you think the woodlice prefer to live in dark, damp places?
- **To focus children's attention on key science ideas**
  Is the end of the tuning fork moving?
  Which kind of birds ate the breadcrumbs from the bird table?
- **To promote the links between science ideas**
  If we have a lot of energy we can run faster. How could you give the car on the slope more energy and what would happen if you did?

Consider the following strategies when using questions in science.

When talking to the whole class:

- **Encourage all children to attempt an answer by asking a question then waiting a while**

before choosing someone to answer it. Insist on hands up to achieve this.
- Encourage less cooperative children by asking them directly what they think.
- Encourage more children to be involved in giving answers by giving no response after the first answer. This enables others to have a go before knowing which is the acceptable answer.
- Give praise for a correct answer or a partly correct one.
- Give praise for attempting to answer even if the answer is wrong.
- Try to include all children at some time. Do not get into a habit of only asking children near the front or who are more attention-seeking than others.
- Ensure you get a gender balance in the children you ask.

When talking to a group:

- There is more potential here for allowing children to provide answers without hands up but don't be afraid to impose this rule if necessary.
- Give children a chance to respond to each other's answers in a group situation.
- Encourage children to ask questions of one another if possible.
- Take a less formal approach in a small group, if possible, to put the children at ease.

When talking to individuals:

- Put the child at ease as soon as possible. Use humour and encouragement to do this if necessary.
- Use facial expression and body language to encourage responses to questions.
- Don't fire off too many questions at once. Intersperse these with conversation and/or instruction.

Generally:

- Listen to a child's response carefully. Base your next question on what is said and your interpretation of it.
- Make the question easier if a child is struggling.
- Lead a child towards the required answer by asking a series of simpler questions.

Strategies for differentiating work in primary science

See page 62 for more on differentiation

Any group or class of children will be made up of a range of abilities, levels of attainment and personalities. Teachers will therefore always need to consider the differentiation of the work they provide for children. This will involve work which will stretch the more able as well as special tasks or support for the less able. Many teachers prefer to consider children in terms of attainment rather than ability, e.g. high and low attainers rather than more or less able. More able children are not necessarily high attainers, and vice versa, and the terms should be used with care. High expectations of all children regardless of ability or attainment is essential at all times. There is a variety of ways in which teachers can differentiate work in science:

- by preparing work at different ability levels for ability groups within the class;
- by having mixed ability groups in which different tasks are allocated according to ability

or preferred learning style;

- by providing graduated material in which different abilities begin and finish at different points;
- by providing extension work for more able children within the class, to be done once they have achieved the main task;
- by providing extra teaching support for those who are less able and/or those who are more able – for instance by paying more attention to such a group or allocating a classroom assistant to the group;
- by arranging for the more able children to help the less able ones;
- by expecting a different outcome from different groups – this works especially well when the task is an open-ended one such as a problem-solving exercise or a science investigation;
- by using computer-aided learning which has differentiation built into it.
- by modifying and using different resources for different groups.

It would also be a mistake to assume that a child who is of a certain ability in, say, maths or English, will be of a similar ability in all aspects of science. For instance, quite often teachers comment on the fact that children who are of an average ability in most subjects are often particularly able when it comes to some aspects of science, especially practical work. Also children have different preferred learning styles as well as abilities. Thus a child who prefers to express her scientific ideas verbally may not do so well in writing and vice versa. Thus teachers may want to differentiate the way children plan, execute and respond to work in science to suit such characteristics.

Strategies for organising teaching groups

There is a variety of ways of organising groups of children to do science in the classroom. For example:

These are dealt with on page 69, Chapter 7

- One group does science while others do other subjects – enables more attention to be given to the science group.
- All children do same activity as individuals/pairs/groups – enables the teacher to talk to whole class about work in progress.
- Use of the activity circus in which groups do different science activities on a similar theme and then rotate round until all tasks are completed – enables the use of scarce equipment and the build-up of a particular concept through many short activities.
- Each group does a different but related activity (and provides feedback to the whole class) – enables an accumulation of experience within the class within a short time and encourages explanation and discussion.

A SUMMARY OF **KEY POINTS**

> **All activities should lead to a progression in children's learning.**
> **Teachers should have an understanding of the ideas that children bring to science lessons and be prepared to encourage children to challenge and reconsruct these.**
> **Practical activities are an effective way of learning science but not all science can be taught in this way.**

> Non-practical activities such as the use of secondary sources of information, analogy and role-play can play an important part in teaching science.
> The precise use of language plays an important part in the effective learning of science.
> There is a variety of strategies for differentiating work in primary science.
> There is a variety of strategies for effective teacher exposition.
> There is a variety of strategies for effective classroom organisation.
> There is a variety of strategies for employing teacher's questioning.

Moving on

During your induction year you should develop *a good up-to-date working knowledge and understanding of a range of teaching, learning and behaviour management strategies and know how to use and adapt them ...* (Professional Standards for Teachers, I 10). Consider one or two of the teaching strategies described in this chapter which you have not used before. Plan to use these in your next teaching experience.

FURTHER READING   FURTHER READING   FURTHER READING

Arthur, J. et al. (2006) Learning to Teach in the Primary School. Abingdon. Routledge.

Harlen, W. (2000) *Teaching, Learning and Assessing Science 5–12*, 3rd edn. London: Paul Chapman. Chapter 7 on the teacher's role provides good advice on a variety of strategies to be used in the classroom to promote effective learning in science.

Hayes, D. (2000) *The Handbook for Newly Qualified Teachers: Meeting the Standards in Primary and Middle Schools*. London: Fulton.

Peacock, G. A. (2002) *Teaching Science in Primary Schools*. London: Letts. Each chapter gives examples of suitable teaching strategies for primary science topics.

QCA (1998) *Science: a Scheme of Work for Key Stages 1 and 2 – Teacher's Guide*. London: QCA. The teacher's guide provides some brief advice on classroom strategies for implementing the scheme.

REFERENCES   REFERENCES   REFERENCES   REFERENCES   REFERENCES

QCA/DfEE (1998, with amendments 2000) *Science: a Scheme of Work for Key Stages 1 and 2*. London: QCA.

6
Planning

Introduction

This chapter provides an introduction to some of the important considerations to bear in mind when planning science lessons. It does not set out a foolproof way of doing this because teaching is a creative profession where approaches need to be responsive to a wide variety of situations. Teachers may take many of the ideas discussed in this chapter and weave them into a series of learning programmes which suit the children they teach and the resources available for doing this.

This chapter is closely linked to page 36, Chapter 5, on teaching strategies

Levels of planning within a school

Planning is the work you do before the lesson so that it runs smoothly, addresses the learning needs of the children and fits into a wider programme of learning for those children. There are different levels of planning to suit different time scales:

- long-term planning;
- medium-term planning;
- short-term planning.

Long-term planning

At some time, a broad overview or long-term plan of the learning in science for each child throughout the primary school years will be required. In a single primary school, this is often prepared by the science coordinator or subject leader (or a small team of teachers working in conjunction with the whole staff). Long-term plans are often referred to as schemes of work. Schemes of work are based on a school policy for science which is often produced by the science coordinator and/or subject leader. It is debatable which of these two documents actually comes first. In an ideal world, policies are established and everything else builds on that firm basis. In reality, a clear policy will often emerge from current practice which may be based on a partly formed scheme of work.

A scheme of work has a number of features which will help in the formation of effective plans for teaching.

- It will map out briefly what each year group within a school should be studying in science over each term.
- It may show broad learning objectives and learning outcomes for each block of work.
- It may suggest where there should be a particular emphasis in science investigations.
- It may refer to useful resources including the publications available in school.
- It may suggest cross-curricular links.

How a scheme might be used

There are a number of major functions which a scheme will enable the science co-ordinator or subject leader and other teachers to perform. A scheme can be used to ensure:

- coverage of the National Curriculum requirements for science;
- that there is a broad and balanced set of experiences in science;
- that there is suitable progression and continuity in science learning;
- that some science topics are revisited within the primary years;
- that unnecessary repetition is avoided.

Medium-term planning

Medium-term plans enable teachers to gain an overview of a single block of work which may last from two or three hours to a whole term. A medium-term plan contains more detail than a typical scheme of work and will most often be used by a year group team of teachers. A medium-term plan maps out briefly the stages that the children will move through, perhaps on a week by week basis. It contains more detailed learning objectives and learning outcomes which might be achieved over the period of time to which it applies.

Teachers use a medium-term plan as a guide and base their individual lesson plans on this. Features of a medium-term plan include:

- **more specific learning objectives and learning outcomes which would be achieved over a period of time;**
- **links with Programmes of Study from the National Science Curriculum;**
- **brief descriptions of each learning experience perhaps with a suggested time scale for each;**
- **cross-curricular links;**
- **assessment opportunities;**
- **examples of children's activities;**
- **an indication of the resources available for the topic.**

All medium-term and long-term plans should be the subject of constant review by the school. The plans are therefore working documents which are adaptable enough to be changed to keep up with current developments in the subject.

The Scheme of Work for Science at Key Stages 1 and 2

The line between long-term and medium-term plans is rather vague. The exemplar Scheme of Work for primary science (QCA/DfEE, 1998, with amendments 2000), for example, provides an overview of suggested work in science as a series of Units for the whole primary school and yet contains sufficient detail to be used as a single topic planning document. Many schools have now adapted or replaced their own individual schemes of work with the exemplar provided.

In the example shown overleaf, teachers are given a synopsis of the Unit and told where it fits in with in the scheme. It provides a short list of things the children should be able to do before starting work. The vocabulary that will be covered is outlined as are the resources that will be required. The expectations of the children are set out in terms of what most children will achieve by the end of the Unit but also what is expected of 'some children who have not made so much progress' and those who 'have progressed further'.

Inside the cover of the Unit, the learning programme for the seven weeks' work is set out. Broad *Learning objectives* such as 'Children should learn to explain how to make familiar objects move faster or slower' are outlined along with related *Possible teaching activities*. It is suggested, for example, that the teacher takes the children into the playground to enable them to demonstrate ways of slowing things down. It is also suggested that children record their ideas in drawings and in a simple story.

Another section describes *Learning outcomes* which provide pointers for assessing child achievement. For instance, children 'describe how they can make themselves slow down' if they have achieved the learning objective outlined above. A final column, *Points to note*, provides advice to teachers on various aspects of the Unit.

Unit 2E Forces and movement

YEAR 2

ABOUT THE UNIT

The work in this Unit extends children's understanding of how pushes and pulls affect the movement and shape of objects.

Experimental and investigative work focuses on:

• thinking about what is expected to happen

• making measurements

• recording and presenting results and deciding whether the results support the prediction

• deciding whether comparisons are fair.

Children also have opportunities to relate science to the ways in which familiar objects move.

This Unit takes approximately 7 hours.

WHERE THE UNIT FITS IN

Builds on Unit 1E 'Pushes and pulls', and 2D 'Grouping and changing materials'

Children need:

• to be able to describe different kinds of movement

• to know that pushes and pulls can make things start or stop moving

• to have experience of measuring length in standard or non-standard units.

Links with Unit 1C and with physical education.

VOCABULARY

In this Unit children will have opportunities to use:

• words related to movement eg *direction, distance, force*

• comparative expressions eg *further, furthest, fast, faster, fastest, slow, slower, slowest, higher*

• expressions of reason using 'because'

• expressions making predictions.

RESOURCES

• materials such as plasticine or dough

• collection of toy cars and other toys that move

• apparatus for measuring length eg *metre sticks or tape measures*

• bean bags and/or soft balls

• bricks and pieces of wood/thick card to make ramps

• collection of pictures or video clips showing moving objects

• access, if possible, to large moving apparatus

EXPECTATIONS

at the end of this Unit

most children will:

describe how to use pushes and pulls to make familiar objects speed up, slow down, or change direction or shape; recognise that pushes and pulls are forces; plan a comparison and decide whether it was fair; make measurements of length using standard units and present these in a chart

some children will not have made so much progress and will:

describe how to change the movement of familiar objects using pushes and pulls; make measurements of length and compare these

some children will have progressed further and will also:

explain how they made their comparison fair and suggest several factors to investigate

Example of a Unit from the QCA/DfES Scheme of Work for Science

It is clear from this brief description that the scheme provides sufficient material for broad topic planning but would need to be taken further in order to carry out individual lessons on the subject.

Short-term planning

Lesson plans provide guidance for the teacher and communicate to others in the school exactly what is intended to happen in a single lesson. Trainees on school experience will be expected to produce detailed lesson plans in order to communicate their ideas to a wide audience including their class teacher. It is often the first kind of detailed planning that a trainee or newly qualified teacher is involved in because the broader planning will have already been done by others.

Learning objectives

At the heart of a good lesson plan are the learning objectives for that lesson. These are often, but not always, the starting point for detailed short-term plans. (Some schools and local education authorities refer to learning objectives as teaching objectives to distinguish them from learning outcomes.)

In the past many teachers were tempted to begin with identifying an exciting science activity which was certain to interest a group of children, then work 'backwards' to identify the learning objectives which fitted this. Placing the learning objectives second, however, meant that often the same objectives were covered more than once and some important objectives remained neglected. The formation of a scheme of work and topic plan first means that it is essential to begin planning lessons with learning objectives drawn from these.

The table below provides examples of broad learning objectives drawn from the QCA/DfES Scheme of Work together with examples of more specific learning objectives suitable for related lesson plans.

Unit of work	Relevant programme of study statement from National Curriculum for science	Broad learning objective from medium-term plan	Example of a related learning objective
1A Ourselves	Sc2 Life processes and living things 4a Pupils should be taught to recognise similarities and differences between themselves and others.	Children should learn that there are differences between humans.	By the end of the lesson most children should be able to collect and record data on the eye colour of a group of children.
2E Plants and animals in the local environment	Scl Scientific enquiry 2a Pupils should be taught to ask questions and decide how they might find answers to them.	Children should learn to turn ideas of their own, about what plants need to begin to grow, into a form that can be tested.	By the end of the lesson most children should be able to make a list of the things they think a plant needs to grow.
4F Circuits and conductors	Sc3 Materials and their properties lc Pupils should be taught that some materials are better electrical conductors than others.	Children should learn that some materials are better conductors than others.	By the end of the lesson most children should be able to test these six things for conductivity: aluminium foil, steel key, paper, copper ornament, pencil lead, wooden rod.
6C More about dissolving	Scl Scientific enquiry 2c Pupils should be taught to think about what might happen or try things out when deciding what to do, what kind of evidence to collect, and what kind of equipment and materials to use.	Children should learn to make predictions about what happens when water from a solution evaporates and to test these predictions.	By the end of the lesson most children should be able to predict what will happen to the salt solution and should be able to link this prediction to a previous experience.

The relationship between Programmes of Study, objectives for the topic and learning objectives for the lesson.

Learning objectives should be written in a particular way. They should not be broad descriptions of what the teacher will do in the lesson but rather statements of what the teacher wants the children to learn by the end of the lesson. It is often a good idea to begin:

'By the end of the lesson most children should be able to...; know...; understand...'

Teachers will describe what children are intended to achieve in terms of what they should be able to do, to understand or to know.

See page 80, Chapter 8

There need only be about two or three learning objectives for each lesson which provide the main focus of the work. Often more than is required will be achieved. Some teachers like to display the learning objectives on the blackboard or a flip chart for the children to see during the lesson. The importance of clear learning objectives will become apparent when planning to assess the children's understanding.

PRACTICAL TASK PRACTICAL TASK **PRACTICAL TASK** PRACTICAL TASK

Read these extracts from the Programmes of Study in the National Curriculum for primary science. Devise some suitable learning objectives, appropriate for individual lessons, which would be related to each of them.

Key Stage 1

Sc3 Materials and their properties

1b   Children should be taught to sort objects into groups on the basis of simple material properties (for example, roughness, hardness, shininess, ability to float, etc.).

Key Stage 1

Sc1 Scientific enquiry

2h   Children should be taught to make simple comparisons and identify simple patterns or associations.

Key Stage 2

Sc4 Physical processes

3e   Children should be taught that sounds are made when objects (for example, strings on musical instruments) vibrate, but that vibrations are not always directly visible.

Typical lesson plan format

It is often helpful to write lesson plans into a formatted page. Each lesson is different, however, and different amounts of detail will be required in each section. It can also be helpful to use a series of headings and write as much as is necessary under each. A typical lesson plan for science might use the following headings:

TITLE _____

Date/Class and year group/Number of children/Duration

National Science Curriculum and QCA/DfEE Scheme of Work for Science
Refer to the appropriate Programme(s) of Study/and Units of work.
These may include references to the Level Descriptions where appropriate.

Relationship to the school's long-term and medium-term plans
Which part of the school's medium-term plan does this lesson address?
Does it form part of a sequence?

Children's previous experiences
What have most children experienced on a similar subject?

Learning objectives
By the end of the lesson:
– most children should be able to . . .; know . . .; understand . . .
– in addition, more able children should be able to . . .; know . . .; understand . . .
– less able children should be able to . . .; know . . .; understand . . .
Include reference to skills, knowledge and understanding, children's attitudes,
children's spiritual, moral, social and cultural development, etc.

Lesson sequence
Introduction *– set the scene – show how you will relate the work to children's*
    everyday lives.
Child activity *– how will the lesson develop?*
Conclusion *– summarise the key points of the lesson*.

These three basic stages of a lesson might be described in terms of:
(a) What the teacher will do.
(b) What the children will do.
(c) How the children and the classroom will be organised.

Classroom organisation and management
Reference to use of space, whole class/group/individual teaching, approximate
timing of lesson phases/activities, role of teacher and other adults, allocation of
resources.

Differentiation strategies
How will you support those who are less able?
How will you provide extension work for those who need it?
Do individual children have special requirements?

Homework
Is this lesson a basis for setting homework?
What would this be?

Assessment opportunities
Which learning objective(s) will form the basis for your assessment?
Who will you assess?
How will you assess?
What evidence will you gather to support your assessment?
How will you use your assessment in your future plans?

Recording and reporting
How will you record the results of your assessment?
Which aspects of this lesson might be reported to others in the school, parents or the children themselves?

Health and safety
Are there any health and safety issues associated with this lesson?

Not all headings need to be used for every lesson plan. Treat the above as a checklist so that no important piece of information is left out.

Planning for science

Planning for science lessons will involve a number of features which are perhaps not found in other subjects. An important feature for children of primary school age will be a varied approach which is often practical in nature and relates the science ideas to their everyday experiences. Good planning will take account of current ideas about how children learn science as well as how they might learn to 'think like a scientist'.

One of the greatest challenges to teachers of primary science is to understand for themselves the scientific ideas they wish to teach. They often have to know well beyond what they would expect their children to learn. This can pose particular problems for those who teach towards the end of Key Stage 2 where the science becomes ever more sophisticated. There are no easy solutions to this dilemma. Very competent teachers towards the end of their career will still be learning more about even the simplest science ideas that they teach. Training requirements are more rigorous now, however, and this will help significantly.

Primary Science: Knowledge and Understanding (2007) *in this series tackles the issue of science background knowledge for teachers and provides a sound basis for learning more*

Teachers who plan practical activities for children should be wary of the seemingly simple activities described in many books and worksheets. What appears to be straightforward on the printed page can often become difficult in practice. It is therefore essential when planning activities to try them out practically beforehand. Some of the best primary science planning happens in the kitchen at home! Simply *writing* a lesson plan for a practical task does not guarantee success!

The following sections outline some of the major considerations to be made when planning primary science lessons.

Children's science ideas

Are you aware of the ideas currently held by your children concerning the science you are about to teach?

A great deal of research has been carried out into the ideas that children hold in some of the major areas of science (e.g. the Science Process and Concept Exploration or SPACE Project, the Children's Learning in Science or CLIS Project, and so on). The research has demonstrated that children learn science by building upon what they already know. This is the constructivist view of learning science. When planning a series of science lessons it is often useful to elicit the children's ideas about the science they are to learn first and to consider these ideas carefully. This may have implications for the way a topic or an individual lesson is structured. For instance, before launching into a series of activities on the subject of forces it might be necessary to plan an elicitation task which enables children to express their own ideas. Further planning might then depend on the results of this exercise.

Described in detail on page 25, Chapter 4

Described in detail on page 32, Chapter 4

Lesson structure and pace

Have you thought about how you will adjust the structure and pace of the lesson to suit most of the children?

Lesson structure is made up of the variety of learning activities and the timing of each. It is important to plan for child experiences and teacher intervention. Different groups of children may have differently structured experiences in the same lesson.

For instance, a simple structure for a whole class of Year 4 children might consist of:

- **the lesson introduction 15 minutes**
- **the main child activity 40 minutes**
- **the lesson conclusion 10 minutes**

Many lessons, however, will not (and should not necessarily) conform to this pattern.

IN THE CLASSROOM

Making electrical switches
Miss Taylor wrote her learning objectives for the lesson as follows.

By the end of the lesson most children should:
- be able to find and rectify faults in a simple electrical circuit;
- be able to use two batteries in a circuit to light a bulb;
- know how a variety of handmade switches can be used to control electricity in a circuit.

The Year 3 class had already learnt in the previous lesson how to join a battery to a bulb to make it light and a buzzer to make it buzz. Miss Taylor now wanted to teach her children how to overcome simple problems if their circuits did not work. She gave them each a troubleshooting table and demonstrated each fault to the children.

PROBLEM *Circuit does not work because:*	REMEDY
Bulb is loose in its holder	Screw it down
Bulb is broken	Replace bulb
There is a loose or dirty connection to the bulb holder	Wiggle connector/Clean connector
The crocodile connector is faulty	Replace connector with one which is known to work
The battery is loose in its holder	Wiggle battery
One battery is the wrong way round	Turn battery
The battery is dead	Replace with battery known to be working
The buzzer is the wrong way round	Change buzzer connections

The children were then allowed 10 minutes to make a simple circuit with two batteries in a holder and a bulb or buzzer. While they were doing this, Miss Taylor went around to each group and 'sabotaged' their circuits by unscrewing a bulb, changing one battery round or making some buzzer connections a little loose! She made it clear that it was the responsibility of the children to try to rectify any faulty circuits whenever they had problems.

The children were then asked to watch while Miss Taylor showed them how to make some simple switches for their circuits using aluminium foil, paper clips and card. A worksheet was produced with a number of different switch designs on it and the children set to work to make as many as they could in the time available.

At the end of the lesson some children were able to demonstrate their completed switches in their bulb or buzzer circuit.

The structure for Miss Taylor's lesson enabled her to make two 'introductions' – one to discuss troubleshooting and the second to demonstrate making switches. She used a brisk pace for the first part because she knew the children would come back to the idea of troubleshooting throughout their work on electricity. She allowed more time for making a variety of switches thus enabling the work to be differentiated. This was achieved by increasing the difficulty of each switch described on the worksheet and expecting all children to make the easier ones first.

Introducing a science lesson

Do you begin your science lessons in a variety of ways?

Consider beginning the lesson by adopting one or more of the following:

- **recapping on the previous lesson;**
- **reading a story to set the scene;**
- **showing a picture or poster;**
- **discussing an artefact you have brought to school, e.g. a push-along toy for a topic on forces;**
- **watching a short video or using a CD-ROM presentation;**

- referring to an out-of-school visit the children have recently made;
- taking the children for a short trip around the school, for instance to look at the use of building materials;
- demonstrating a scientific phenomenon such as a paper helicopter dropped in front of the children;
- asking children for their experiences of a relevant topic such as examples of materials which are waterproof;
- eliciting children's ideas about the way shadows are formed during the day by asking them to make a poster;
- asking children to begin by 'playing' with, for instance, a collection of magnets to find out whatever they can.

Children's activities

Do you vary the kind of learning activity experienced by the children?

In the development of the lesson, children might spend most of their time on activities such as:

- careful observation of an object or collection of things such as seeds or rocks;
- drawing, discussing or describing in writing the things they have observed;
- doing something practical by following instructions which might be presented verbally, on a workcard, worksheet or the blackboard/whiteboard;
- using role-play to help understand a science idea;
- planning and carrying out a science investigation;
- recording and interpreting scientific results;
- reporting their findings and conclusions to others – verbally, in writing, through drawings, etc.;
- completing a worksheet by responding with written answers and drawings, etc.
- completing a quiz;
- using secondary sources of information to learn new ideas, e.g. using posters, reference books, CD-ROM, TV or video programmes or the internet;
- asking questions.

Concluding the lesson

Do you vary the way in which you bring a lesson to a close?

Children are often willing to pay special attention towards the end of the lesson so this is a good opportunity to consolidate teaching. Also, this time gives the teacher a chance to praise good work and reinforce good practices. You might conclude a lesson by:

- summarising the science the children have been learning;
- showing examples of successful work by some children;
- extending the children's learning by asking suitable questions;
- asking children to explain some of their ideas or describe what they have been doing;
- collecting together the results of a class investigation;
- challenging some of the misunderstandings that may have arisen during the lesson;
- discussing what the children will be doing next in the sequence of lessons.

Practical activities

Do your children develop their science ideas through simple practical activity?

There is a strong tradition that learning in science in the primary school is often achieved through practical work. Not all ideas are best learnt through practical science activities but the nature of the subject is such that these often play a more important role than in many other subjects. Practical work requires special planning skills which consider the distribution and maintenance of resources, time management and lesson structure. There are no hard and fast rules, but the following are worth thinking about before planning a practical lesson:

- **Do the children understand how to behave in a practical activity situation? Do they need special instructions in this respect?**
- **How much time in the lesson should be spent on practical work?**
- **Is it appropriate to use teacher demonstration for part of the time?**
- **Should the teacher control the practical work by having individual children demonstrate to the class?**
- **Should children work alone or in groups?**
- **How should learning be consolidated during or after the practical activity?**
- **Which kind of practical work best suits the learning objectives?**
- **How should instructions be provided so that the children can work independently?**
- **Should extension work be provided for those who finish early?**
- **What special help will some children need?**
- **How will equipment be cleared away?**
- **What should be done about faulty equipment during the lesson?**
- **How should children record their ideas and procedures?**
- **How should the learning be summarised?**
- **What assessment opportunities will arise?**

Preparing to ask questions

See page 45 for more on asking questions

Do you promote effective learning by asking a variety of types of question to individuals, groups and the whole class?

One of the most important and effective ways to teach primary science is to ask appropriate questions of the children. It is often possible to plan a set of key questions which might be used as a stimulus to asking further questions during the lesson. Asking a string of appropriate and challenging questions 'off the top of one's head' is not easy and this is a skill which takes time to acquire. It helps to think of the different categories that teachers' questions might fall into and to plan to ask a variety of different types. Consider these examples on the subject of light and colour.

- **Where does light come from?**
- **Name two things that give out their own light.**
- **Tell me some things you can think of which are shiny.**
- **Which is your favourite colour?**
- **Do you think you can see in the dark?**
- **What are the colours of the rainbow?**
- **How long does it take light to reach us from the sun?**

- What happens to light when it is reflected from a mirror?
- Do you think light can pollute the environment?
- How do you know the colours you see are the same as anyone else?

Some of these questions require a direct, factual answer. We could describe these as *closed questions*. Some questions, however, require a more expansive answer which may include personal opinion. These could be described as *open-ended questions*. Notice that some questions have neither a correct nor incorrect answer. Teachers should plan to ask a variety of types of questions while avoiding the trap of asking only closed questions because these appear more 'scientific'.

Closed questions:

- test specific recall;
- can be used to assess knowledge, understanding and prior learning;
- require only a limited response (e.g. a one-word answer);
- could be perceived as threatening to a child;
- could be avoided by a child who claims to be unable to answer.

Open-ended questions:

- elicit a range of responses – some surprising!
- can be less threatening than closed questions;
- elicit a longer, fuller and often more revealing response than closed questions;
- are less likely to be avoided by a child.

REFLECTIVE TASK
REFLECTIVE TASK

Consider the following questions a teacher might ask on the subject of electricity. Decide which questions are closed and which are open. Do all questions fit neatly into these categories? Which questions would you find threatening?

1. Can you think of some things which use electricity?
2. What do we call the thing we use in the classroom which gives us electricity?
3. What is inside a torch bulb?
4. If I tie a knot in a wire in an electrical circuit what do you think will happen to the brightness of the bulb?
5. What name do we give to the pushing power of a battery?
6. Electricity can be used to make heat. What else can it do?
7. What do you think electricity is?
8. If electricity is like the flow of water in a pipe how could we show the effect of putting a light bulb in the circuit?
9. Do you think living near electricity pylons is good for your health?
10. What would the world be like without electricity?

You can read more about asking appropriate questions in science on page 45, Chapter 5

You can read more about differentiation on page 46, Chapter 5

Differentiation

Is it necessary to differentiate by task or by outcome some of the work in the lesson to cater for less able and more able children?

Part of a successful plan for a science lesson will involve some suggestion for catering for different abilities or levels of attainment within a group or class. An example of such provision would be planned extension work for those who finish early. A different kind of extension may be devised for those who are particularly able. These children may not necessarily finish early but may need directing towards something more challenging. Less able children may need different instructions or different work to do. Alternatively you may plan to provide extra help for them as they complete the work that most will do. In some instances, work may be differentiated by accepting different outcomes from a task. This might be true for a group of children who are given an open-ended task of planning a simple investigation. The more able children might be expected to produce a more sophisticated plan. Some children may have preferred learning styles within a class such as a preference for discussing ideas rather than writing them down.

Progression

Does the work you have planned enable children to move on from their current knowledge and understanding? Does it link to what they know already?

Children should progress in:

- **their knowledge and understanding of science concepts;**
- **their ability to carry out scientific enquiry.**

The issue of progression is often dealt with at the long- or medium-term planning stage. Broad features of progression in primary science include children moving from:

- **using everyday language to increasingly precise use of technical and scientific vocabulary, notation and symbols**
  I pulled the toy to make it move along ⟶ *A force was necessary to make it turn a corner.*
- **personal scientific knowledge in a few areas to understanding in a wider range of areas and of links between areas**
  I know puddles dry faster in the playground when it is windy ⟶ *Puddles dry through evaporation in the same way that clothes dry on a line, cakes go stale and paint dries.*
- **describing events and phenomena to explaining events and phenomena**
  The screwed up piece of paper fell faster ⟶ *The screwed up piece of paper fell faster because it had less air resistance.*
- **explaining phenomena in terms of their own ideas to explaining phenomena in terms of accepted ideas or models**
  I can see the clock by aiming my eyes at it ⟶ *Light from the bulb falls on the clock face and is reflected into my eyes.*

- participating in practical science activities to building increasingly abstract models of real situations

  I investigated which kind of leaf the snail preferred to eat ⟶ I understand the food chain which includes the bird which eats the snail which eats the leaf.

  (Adapted from QCA/DfEE, 1998, p. 6)

Progression within individual lessons can be as important as overall progression. Children should move towards the learning objectives of the lesson, beginning with what they already know and understand, towards new ideas. Teachers can facilitate this kind of progression by structuring their lesson into a series of 'digestible chunks' of learning. Every opportunity should be taken to challenge and extend the children's knowledge, understanding and skills (and not simply keep them occupied) through questioning and directed tasks. The conclusion to a lesson is often a time when a teacher might push understanding to its furthest limits.

Assessment and recording

Have you thought about how you will know whether the children have achieved the learning objectives?

See Chapter 8 for a detailed discussion of assessment in science

Planning for assessment is as important as planning what the children will do.

Further considerations in planning science lessons

The following questions complete the checklist for lesson planning.

Cross-curricular links
Are there any links with other subjects that would enhance the science? How will these links be made?

Information and Communications Technology (ICT)
Is there potential for using ICT to support the science learning in this lesson?

See Chapter 9 for a more detailed account of how this might be achieved

ICT might be used by all or some of the children, if this is appropriate, to enhance learning in a part of the lesson.

Vocabulary
Is there a short list of scientific and technical vocabulary which you would like the children to learn to use in this lesson?

You might consider preparing some flash cards with the appropriate words on them.

Classroom assistants
Have you made plans for the role of any assistants you may have in the classroom? How will you communicate these ideas to the assistant?

Evaluating the lesson

Part of a good planning strategy is to reflect on what happened in a lesson and record a written evaluation. This is not the same as the assessment of children's achievements. Child assessment, however, might be used to inform the lesson evaluation. It is a good idea to focus on different areas of the teaching in each evaluation in order to target specific aspects for improvement. Each evaluation might contain some or all of the following elements:

TITLE_____

Date/Class and year group/Number of children/Duration

The children's performance
Was the content of the lesson appropriate and stimulating for most children?
Did the planned work stretch the children in their educational development?
How did the children respond to the lesson? (Refer to the learning objectives if this is appropriate.)
What were the reasons for their response?
Did the children learn what was intended?
Did any children fail to benefit (e.g. able children, average children, less able children, shy children, female/male children, disruptive children, etc.)? If so why?

My performance as a teacher
What went well? Why was this so?
What could have been improved?
Did you work well with other adults in the classroom?

Lessons for the future
What have you learnt about the subject content?
What have you learnt about the way to deliver this subject?
What have you learnt about the way children learn?

Targets from previous lesson evaluations
Have you achieved any targets that you have previously set yourself?

Targets for the future
Set yourself two or three personal targets to aim for when teaching in the future.

A SUMMARY OF **KEY POINTS**

> **Planning effective learning programmes takes place at three different levels:**
  – **long-term plans often made by the subject leader;**
  – **medium-term plans often made by the subject leader and year group team;**
  – **short-term 'lesson' plans made by the class teacher.**
> **Long-term and medium-term plans may merge into one scheme of work.**
> **Lesson plans should begin with clear learning objectives.**
> **Key elements in a lesson plan include:**
  – **adopting a suitable structure and pace;**
  – **finding out children's science ideas;**
  – **designing suitable activities for the children;**
  – **asking effective questions;**
  – **differentiated work;**
  – **assessment opportunities.**
> **Trainees should reflect on their lessons by evaluating them and setting targets for future lessons.**

Moving on

During your induction year you should plan and teach *... challenging, well-orga-nised lessons ... that take account of the prior learning and attainment ... of your pupils* (Professional Standards for Teachers, I 26). Talk to individual children about their understanding of science topics. Consider how you would enhance the under-standing of these children.

FURTHER READING   FURTHER READING   FURTHER READING

Arthur, J. et al. (2006) *Learning to Teach in the Primary School*. Abingdon: Routledge.

Harlen, W. (2000) *Teaching, Learning and Assessing Science 5–12,* 3rd edn. London: Paul Chapman Publishing. A good general introduction to planning science lessons. Particularly strong on assessment.

Harlen, W. (2004) *The Teaching of Science in Primary Schools*. London: Fulton.

Hayes, D. (2000) *The Handbook for Newly Qualified Teachers: Meeting the Standards in Primary and Middle Schools*. London: Fulton.

Peacock, G. A. (1999) *Teaching Science in Primary Schools*. London: Letts. Provides a wealth of ideas to use in the classroom in a structured science programme.

REFERENCES REFERENCES **REFERENCES** REFERENCES REFERENCES

QCA/DfEE (1998, with amendments 2000) *Science: a Scheme of Work for Key Stages 1 and 2*. London: QCA.

QCA (1998) *Science: a Scheme of Work for Key Stages 1 and 2 – Teachers' Guide*. London: QCA.

7
Classroom organisation and management

For more information on planning, see Chapter 6

Introduction

Science lessons must be organised and managed carefully and skilfully if effective science teaching and learning are to take place. The range of organisational and management strategies available for use when planning and teaching primary science are wide ranging and sometimes difficult and complex decisions have to be made when selecting those strategies considered best suited to and fit for the purposes intended. Critical reflection and analysis of the organisational and management strategies employed in science lessons will help to identify areas for improvement and help to inform future planning. Though different things, organisation and management are completely interdependent. It is important to be good at both.

RESEARCH SUMMARY RESEARCH SUMMARY **RESEARCH SUMMARY**

Most authors agree that while there is no one way of organising and managing all lessons within all primary classrooms, there are several features of classroom organisation and management which are associated with good practice and which are recognised to contribute towards effective teaching and learning as a whole (e.g. Alexander et al., 1992; Ofsted, 1993; Hayes, 2003, 2004). Within the context of primary science, a range of strategies have been described in more detail (e.g. Harlen and Jelly, 1997; Harlen, 2006; Feasey, 1998; Hollins, 1998). In brief, successful science lessons are most likely to result from a mixture of whole class, group and individual teaching, having only a small number of groups engaged in science activity at any one time, selecting an appropriate classroom layout and making good use of space, good time management, good behaviour management, and considering carefully the role of the teacher and other adults. The use of computers and display are also important.

The organisation and management of primary science can vary as much from class to class as from school to school. Such variation simply reflects how different teachers (and trainees) respond to the different circumstances they find themselves in and have to deal with on a day-to-day basis (e.g. age and previous science experiences of the children, teaching environments), how each school chooses to present and teach the science curriculum as a whole (e.g. fully integrated topics, science-based topics, subjects) and the diverse nature of schools themselves (e.g. when built, location, physical layout). In this chapter, organisation and management are considered in terms of:

- **teaching the whole class, groups and individuals;**
- **classroom layout and space;**
- **time;**
- **resources;**
- **behaviour;**
- **computers;**
- **display;**
- **role of the teacher and other adults.**

The whole class, groups and individuals

Organising and managing the whole class, groups or individuals depends to a large extent on how as well as what you want children to learn. Throughout the primary years, increasing use is being made of science lessons which are planned and taught within well defined lesson phases. These phases commonly include an introduction, a main science activity (or activities) and a plenary/review. The use of lesson phases is both efficient and effective and ensures that a mixture of whole-class, group and individual teaching takes place.

See also Teaching Strategies, Chapter 5

Whole-class science teaching can eliminate some of the repetition involved when working only with groups. Whole-class science teaching is particularly suited to:

- **the introductory and plenary phases of lessons (e.g. setting the scene, instructing, demonstrating, explaining, reviewing, sharing, discussing, concluding work);**
- **questioning and eliciting ideas (e.g. finding out what children already know and the nature of their errors and misconceptions);**
- **sharing science texts and reading together (e.g. 'big books', researching in libraries);**
- **emphasising matters associated with health and safety (e.g. breakages, spillages, accident and emergency routines);**
- **educational broadcasts (e.g. using television to access or extend science that cannot be undertaken in the classroom).**

When teaching the whole class, firm rules need to be established for determining who is allowed to talk and when (e.g. hands in the air, listening to and respecting the views of others). Teachers (and trainees) also need to consider their position and movement within the classroom or teaching area (e.g. fixed or mobile), teaching style (e.g. formal, informal) and how to keep the children involved and motivated (e.g. interaction). Good board and overhead projector skills are an asset. Transitions from whole-class teaching to group work and back need to be carefully controlled to avoid lost time and disruption.

Group work is perhaps best suited to the main phases of science lessons and would normally, though not necessarily, be expected to follow on naturally from whole class introductions. Grouping allows children to work together collaboratively in organised social settings. The number of groups within a class of children and the number of children within each group may vary but should always be easily manageable. Four or five groups, each with between six and eight children, are particularly common. Group composition is usually determined on the basis of attainment, friendship, control or a mixture of all of these. Typical arrangements include:

- **all groups working on the same science activity at the same time – a variation of whole class teaching (easy to monitor, intervene and control, requires high resource availability, allows for differentiation by task or by outcome);**
- **all groups working on different science activities and sharing findings – (reasonably easy to monitor, intervene and control, requires moderate resource availability, promotes communication skills);**
- **all groups working on different science activities in rotation – sometimes referred to as a circus of activities (good control of rotation essential, requires moderate resource availability, activities should not be linked in terms of sequence or progression, time on activities restricted);**
- **only one group working on science – rest of the class working on other things (useful if science activity needs close supervision or attention, requires low resource availability, monitoring behaviour and quality of work in other groups may be challenging).**

It is essential when working with groups not to be over ambitious at the expense of depth of coverage of the science being taught or to allow the science to lose its distinctiveness, particularly if teaching within fully integrated topics. Careful planning for all forms of group work is required.

All teachers (and trainees) should spend quality time, no matter how short, with each and every child throughout the school day. In science, individual teaching is most likely to occur during the main activity phases of lessons. Working with individuals is particularly useful for monitoring progress, sorting out difficulties perhaps associated with using equipment, collecting, interpreting, analysing and representing data, and clarifying ideas. Working with individuals also helps to strengthen relationships and to build bonds. Children not only receive individual help, they can ask questions and converse in less formal ways without feeling intimidated or humiliated by peers.

REFLECTIVE TASK

Reflect critically and analytically on your own experiences of teaching science to a whole class, groups and individuals. In terms of efficiency and effectiveness, consider the advantages and disadvantages of each way of working. Would efficiency and effectiveness have been affected if you had worked any differently? Can you think of any aspects of science teaching which are better suited to one particular way of working (e.g. effective exposition including questioning, instructing, demonstrating and explaining, skills, concepts and attitudes development, using models and analogies, particular aspects of scientific enquiry, life processes and living things, materials and their properties, physical processes)?

Classroom layout and space

For most teachers (and trainees), science will usually be taught in a classroom or other teaching area. Sometimes, science is taught elsewhere (e.g. in the hall, in corridors, in a special science room, a kitchen, outdoors). Factors which may affect or influence the layout of classrooms and other teaching areas include the size and shape of the space available, the age and number of children present, the amount of furniture required, and the location of exits, storage and resource areas, sinks, boards and windows. Teachers (and trainees) usually begin by experimenting with different layouts to find which works best for most teaching situations – not only science. Freedom of movement around the room and clear lines of sight are essential. Moving furniture for every lesson is not always possible or convenient. This takes time and can cause disruption. Four common layouts include:

- **simple groups;**
- **horseshoes;**
- **rows and columns;**
- **mixed arrangements.**

Many classrooms and teaching areas adopt workstations. Science workstations help contextualise work, focus children's attention and concentration, and provide ready access to resources.

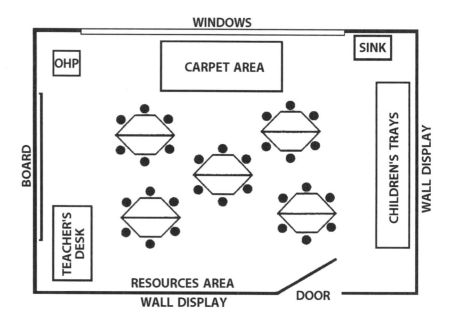

Figure 7.1 Simple groups

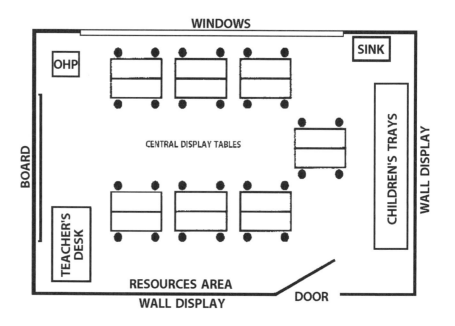

Figure 7.2 Horseshoe

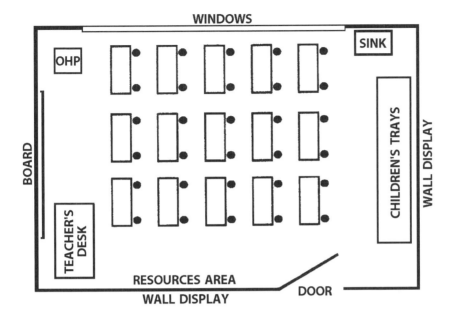

Figure 7.3 Rows and columns

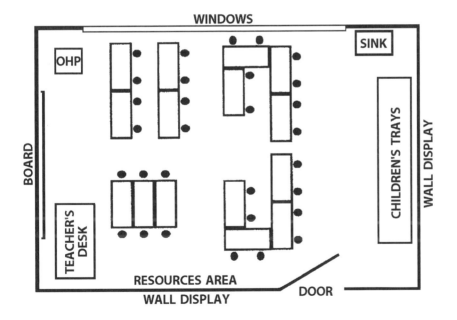

Figure 7.4 Mixed arrangement

Examine each of the classroom layouts on pages 70 and 71. Consider the similarities and differences between these and what you have seen in schools. In terms of advantages and disadvantages, which layouts are best suited to whole-class, group and individual teaching or all three? Which layouts make best use of space and allow for good eye contact and overall class control? Which layouts are best suited to teaching science in Key Stage 1 and Key Stage 2 or both? Does layout matter if teaching about life processes and living things, materials and their properties and physical processes? Which layout do you prefer and why? Given the opportunity, and the year group of your choice, how would you arrange your own classroom?

Time

Time is a valuable commodity in primary science, a commodity which cannot easily be replaced. This is worth remembering when some science investigations or experiments go badly wrong and need to be redone or take much longer to complete than originally anticipated. The time allocated to individual science lessons in primary schools can vary from as little as 30 minutes to as much as 90 minutes or more per week. It is important to realise, however, that within that time, children usually have to be settled, lessons have to be introduced and brought to a satisfactory conclusion, activities have to be completed, classrooms or teaching areas have to be tidied up, and equipment has to be returned. Careful planning, keeping an eye on the clock and experience really do help. It is also worth remembering that not all of the time spent in school is spent teaching. Avoid wasting time:

- **always be thoroughly prepared and ensure that the resources needed for the lesson are readily available;**
- **ensure that the teaching methods selected match the requirements of the lesson;**
- **maintain pace, focus and direction and do not become distracted;**
- **be aware of the rate at which different children work and what they can and cannot do;**
- **work to ensure that children spend as much time as possible on-task;**
- **note when other teaching and non-teaching duties may interfere with teaching time.**

Don't forget that time will also be required for marking, assessing and discussing work, revision and keeping records.

Resources

It is often said that high quality science teaching requires high quality resources. While this is undoubtedly true, high quality resources can only improve the quality of science teaching if they are readily available, appropriate for the task at hand and used effectively. While many commercially available science resources are more sophisticated now than ever before, they can also be very expensive. Many high quality science resources are simply collected by teachers (and trainees) or made when needed. Science resources include:

- **items of scientific equipment (e.g. for measuring length, time, volume, mass, temperature and force, magnifiers, magnets, mirrors and lenses, batteries and bulbs, weather boards, models, safety goggles, disposable gloves, and so on);**

- a range of different materials (e.g. paper, textiles, wood, glass, plastics, and so on);
- science schemes including worksheets and workcards (e.g. Nuffield, Ginn, Bath);
- educational broadcasts (e.g. BBC, Channel 4);
- audio tapes, video tapes, slides (e.g. commercially available);
- books (e.g. fiction, non-fiction, 'big books');
- computers (e.g. word processors, CD-ROMs, databases, sensors, control);
- museums and science centres (e.g. education officers, lending facilities);
- the local environment (e.g. school grounds, parks, beaches);
- guest speakers (e.g. parents, professional scientists).

Most of the commonly used science resources listed above are to be found in schools on a permanent basis. Typical arrangements include:

- central storage;
- topic boxes;
- class sets.

In large primary schools, Key Stage 1 and Key Stage 2 resources may be held separately. Most resources are usually well labelled, safe to use and up to date.

Central storage systems keep all science resources together in a designated area. This might be a storage cupboard, part of a corridor or an unused classroom. Storage space is kept to a minimum, access is possible to all teachers at all times, and resource duplication is minimised thus saving money for a wider range of resources. Central storage systems located far from classrooms and other teaching areas may, however, inhibit spontaneous work in science, particularly if teachers (and trainees) are unable to retrieve what they need and school rules require that children may only do so under supervision. Careful curriculum planning is also essential to avoid demand for the same resources at the same time. Topic boxes store everything needed for a particular topic! Topic boxes may be kept together in central storage or, alternatively, in classrooms where they are most needed. Resources may be retained for the duration of a topic and any additional items collected along the way can be added to the collection. Topic boxes may require some resource duplication, perhaps at considerable cost. Topic boxes may also have to be shared between two or more parallel year groups. Class sets ensure that each class has what it needs to deliver the science being taught throughout the year. This allows for immediate and unrestricted access. Resource duplication may be excessive and maintenance costs may be high.

PRACTICAL TASK PRACTICAL TASK **PRACTICAL TASK** PRACTICAL TASK

At the start of your next school placement you should familiarise yourself with the range of science resources available and how these are organised and managed. In terms of the science to be taught, consider carefully what you need, what is available and, as a result, what you must obtain. What are the advantages and disadvantages of the resource organisation and management strategies adopted by the school?

Teaching children how to identify the resources they need, how to look after them and use them safely, and how to collect and return them by themselves is also important. This not only develops a sense of responsibility, it helps lead children towards becoming independent learners. It also saves teaching time. Just as it is important to plan for progression in scientific knowledge and understanding, it is also important to plan for progression in the selection and use of resources. By the end of Key Stage 1, for example, children should be familiar with and able to use an appropriate range of scientific equipment with some help from their teacher. By the end of Key Stage 2, for example, children should be familiar with and able to use a wider range of scientific equipment by themselves. They should know that different pieces of scientific equipment have specific functions, recognise the importance of precision and accuracy in measurements and, where a selection of items is available, be able to choose the best for the task at hand.

IN THE CLASSROOM

Jenny was coming to the end of her first term of teaching with a class of seven year olds. When she first arrived, she naturally fell into the system operated by the school and the other year group teachers around her. Despite successful teaching practices in similar environments during training, things were not going well, particularly with science. The quality of work being produced by the children was lower than expected and Jenny was worried. Jenny raised this issue with her mentor who very wisely suggested that she consider other ways of working but which didn't disrupt the practice of her colleagues. The first thing Jenny did was to reduce the number of groups she taught from six to four, to be made up on the basis of broad levels of attainment rather than friendship. Next, she identified an area of the open-plan teaching area which she easily transformed into a science workstation. The school was well resourced for science and kitting out the workstation did not present any particular problems. Finally, Jenny shifted emphasis from only teaching science in groups to operating a lesson phase system similar to that used in literacy and numeracy. After only a few weeks, Jenny noticed considerable improvements. Not only was the quality of science much better (teaching and learning), the children seemed to be enjoying their new way of working, and Jenny felt happier too! Jenny's mentor, a wise and experienced teacher, gave her the opportunity of sharing her changes during an after-school meeting. Her other year group colleagues were so impressed they agreed to try them out for themselves.

Behaviour

Maintaining order and a good standard of discipline during science lessons is particularly important, not only to secure effective teaching and learning, but to ensure that all matters associated with health and safety are observed and that preventable accidents and injuries are avoided. Establishing clear rules and routines and setting high expectations for behaviour is essential. Children can misbehave and become disruptive during science for any number of different reasons:

- **lessons are badly organised and managed (e.g. unsatisfactory classroom layout and use of space, noise levels too high, transitions sloppy, inadequate time to complete activities, unsuitable resources);**

- groupings are inappropriate;
- the science is too easy or too hard;
- intervention and supervision are inadequate.

Signs of misbehaviour and disruption can soon become all too obvious. Children may talk out of turn, not pay attention, stray around the room, interfere with others, or fail to get on with and finish work. Ways of dealing with minor incidents include:

- eye contact;
- signalling gestures;
- varying use of voice;
- issuing specific commands;
- praise and positive reinforcement.

Serious breaches of discipline may require more serious action to be taken. This should be undertaken in accordance with the school's behaviour policy. Whatever happens, always stay calm and composed and try to avoid confrontation at all costs. Do not be afraid to stop a lesson, particularly if it is felt that health and safety are compromised.

Computers

The use of computers (and other forms of ICT) is expected in all primary schools. It is important that all teachers (and trainees) be familiar with the hardware and software available to support the teaching and learning of science. Typical computer arrangements include:

For more information on using ICT in science, see Chapter 9

- a computer room or suite;
- a cluster of computers (usually along corridors or in specific locations around a school);
- a single computer in a classroom or other teaching area.

A computer room or suite is useful for whole-class teaching but access may be restricted to particular times in any given week or term. Site licences for specific items of software can be expensive. Children may lose sight of the science in their enthusiasm to use the computers. A cluster of computers is useful for group teaching but access may still be restricted. The location of the cluster may require the teacher (and trainee) to be out of the classroom or away from the teaching area for long periods of time. Single computers are useful for up to three children at one time. Access is almost unrestricted. Site licences for specific software items may not be required but a duplication of software may be necessary for use elsewhere in the school at the same time. Monitoring work and ensuring equal access can be problematic and a rota system may be required.

Overall, the use of computers requires teachers (and trainees) to be aware of security (e.g. personal databases), unrestricted Internet access (e.g. unsuitable websites), and health and safety (e.g. keeping loose cables stored tidily, prohibiting food and drink being brought near computers, avoiding adverse lighting and screen glare, ensuring proper tables and chairs are used, avoiding repetitive strain injury, and so on).

Display

Displays are expected in all primary schools. Whatever the age of the children involved, all displays should be big, bold, colourful, informative and interactive. They should also be kept simple and uncluttered. Good science displays:

- **recognise and reward children's efforts;**
- **develop self-esteem;**
- **help generate more purposeful and stimulating classrooms and teaching areas in which to work;**
- **can be used to revise, consolidate and extend learning;**
- **promote science.**

Presentation should always be of the highest quality. Titles and other headings should be clear and legible (e.g. handwritten, cut from paper or card, word-processed) and all work should be single or double mounted where appropriate. Wall mounted displays are probably most common and easiest to produce. Displays on table tops and other work surfaces together with mobiles suspended from ceilings are also popular. Displays should be changed on a regular basis in order to reflect the science work being undertaken and always taken down or replaced when looking tired. Creating science displays can be time-consuming and resource intensive. Forward planning and a sketch are recommended. Children should be fully involved in the overall design and preparation of displays where possible. Mini-displays can also be used to remind children of scientific vocabulary, how to write scientific reports, how to use scientific equipment properly, the steps in a scientific investigation or experiment and health and safety.

Figure 7.5 Interactive displays enhance teaching and learning

Role of the teacher and other adults

At the start of every science lesson it is essential that teachers (and trainees) know exactly what their role and the roles of any other adults present will be. While working with other adults in the classroom or teaching area is now commonplace, it is worth remembering that all teachers are ultimately responsible for everything that goes on at all times. Other adults may include:

- **parent helpers present on a purely voluntary basis;**
- **fully trained and paid learning support assistants;**
- **other teachers including special educational needs coordinators;**
- **guests and visitors.**

Decisions need to be made in advance about when different individuals become involved in the lesson, the extent to which they participate, which groups or individuals they work with and for how long, and what other work they are doing if not directly involved in teaching. This will help to avoid ambiguity, minimise duplication of effort and prevent confusion among children. Establishing positive working relationships and clear lines of communication is essential. Do not expect any help with teaching science beyond the level of expertise or training of the other adults present.

A SUMMARY OF **KEY POINTS**

> **There is no one way of organising and managing all science lessons within all primary classrooms or teaching areas.**
> **The organisation and management of primary science can vary as much from class to class as from school to school.**
> **Organisation and management is as much about how as about what you expect children to learn.**
> **Primary schools make increasing use of well-defined lesson phases incorporating a mixture of whole-class, group and individual science teaching.**
> **Other features of classroom organisation and management which are associated with good practice and which are recognised to contribute towards effective science teaching and learning include appropriate classroom layout and good use of space, good use of time, appropriate selection and use of resources, good control, use of computers, displays, and the carefully considered role of the teacher and other adults.**

Moving on

As you make the transition from your course of initial teacher training into your induction period and NQT year you should continue to monitor, evaluate, reflect upon and review how you organise and manage your classroom to ensure effective teaching and learning. Do not assume that your initial preferred mode of working will turn out to be the best or last the pace. Analyse your practice carefully and always be prepared to adjust it accordingly. Take some time with your induction tutor or mentor to visit other classrooms and observe how things are set out and done there. Walk around the school and take in just how classrooms and more public displays are constructed and presented. Much of what you do may turn out to be beyond your control (school policy or curriculum driven). But always be prepared to try out new ways of working where you can.

FURTHER READING FURTHER READING FURTHER READING

Ward, H., Roden, J., Hewlett, C. and Foreman, J. (2005) *Teaching Science in the Primary Classroom*. London: Paul Chapman.

REFERENCES REFERENCES REFERENCES REFERENCES REFERENCES

Alexander, R., Rose, J. and Woodhead, C. (1992) *Curriculum Organisation and Classroom Practice in Primary Schools: A Discussion Paper*. London: HMSO.

Feasey, R. (1998) *Primary Science Equipment*. Hatfield: ASE.

Harlen, W. (2006) *Teaching, Learning and Assessing Science 5–12.* London: Sage.

Harlen, W. and Jelly, S. (1997) *Developing Science in the Primary Classroom*. Harlow: Longman.

Hayes, D. (2003) *Planning, Teaching and Class Management in Primary Schools*. London: Fulton.

Hayes, D. (2004) *Foundations of Primary Teaching*. London: Fulton.

Hollins, M. (1998) 'Resources for teaching science', in R. Sherrington (ed.), *ASE Guide to Primary Science Education*. Hatfield: ASE, pp. 206–15.

Ofsted (1993) *Curriculum Organisation and Classroom Practice in Primary Schools: A Follow-up Report*. London: HMSO.

8
Assessment, recording and reporting

Introduction

There is an old adage that a pig does not get heavier because it is weighed frequently. Similarly, children do not become better educated simply because they are tested often. Assessment and testing has to contribute to the knowledge and skills of the child being assessed. The distinction between monitoring the curriculum and assessing children needs to be clear. Monitoring is an essential part of record-keeping where the teacher checks what is happening in the class and notes what has been covered. So when monitoring science a teacher may note the coverage of scientific topics. Monitoring may also involve checking the standardisation of assessment levels across the school. This can be done quickly and easily if each class teacher in a school compiles a fairly slim file of science representative of the work done by children in her class. These pieces of information should be annotated with the National Curriculum level and a short justification for this level. Probably the most useful publication to assist inexperienced teachers in this regard is SCAA (1995), which includes a compilation of accurately levelled science work.

For more on evaluation, see page 63, Chapter 6

Good assessment strategies help children to see where they are making progress in their learning and where they are enjoying success. It should also highlight areas where they are still confused. Similarly, if a teacher is to know which strategies encourage effective learning she will need to know about the efficacy of different ways of teaching. This evaluative assessment is of great importance in providing teachers with information about the progress made by children and in allowing comparisons between the success of teaching approaches. At a whole school level schools must be able to set themselves benchmarks for improvement, as suggested in DfES (2007), and assessment of children provides one of the best ways in which progress towards school improvement targets can be measured.

For more on asking questions for assessment, see page 60, Chapter 6

Teachers carry out informal assessment of children as part of their day-to-day routine. This style of assessment is not planned for or recorded, for example where a teacher checks that a child has recorded the reading shown on a thermometer accurately and helps them to read it correctly. On the other hand formal assessment is planned for and sometimes recorded. The term formal assessment should not conjure up images of tests – it usually simply means that the teacher has decided beforehand to assess a particular aspect of learning in one of the variety of ways suggested below. This chapter examines the purposes of assessment and the strategies, which can be used to carry out formal assessment. Methods of keeping a record of children's progress are discussed and the ways in which information is reported are analysed.

Types and function of assessment

Assessment has four main functions. These are to inform:

- **the current teacher about planning for future teaching;**
- **children about their own learning and progress;**
- **subsequent teachers about children's learning and progress;**
- **parents about learning and progress.**

The first two of these are generally achieved through formative assessment, while the second two are generally the result of summative assessment. Formative assessment gives evidence that helps to develop a programme of teaching while summative assessment gives evidence of the child's level of achievement at a particular time.

Formative assessment

Before discussing formative assessment in the classroom we need to briefly consider diagnostic assessment as a type of formative assessment. Diagnostic assessment is most often done by experts in a particular field and focuses on the analysis of deep learning difficulties. Summary results of diagnostic assessment done by specialist agencies are often used by teachers to help inform their work. Diagnostic assessment is not covered in this short chapter as it is rarely possible for a teacher running a busy classroom to have the time or experience to do this effectively.

Formative assessment, which is carried out by class teachers, informs the next step in teaching children and also informs children about their own progress. Teachers need to know what their children understand and how they learn before they begin to teach them. This avoids wasteful repetition or teaching children ideas and skills that are beyond their ability to learn. Once this information has been established teachers need to find ways to measure how much of what they teach results in children learning. This has two benefits:

- **the rate of progress through the work can be adjusted to suit the class or parts of the class;**
- **the teacher can evaluate the effectiveness of different teaching strategies.**

For more on differentiation, see page 46, Chapter 5

IN THE CLASSROOM

Here we look at how one teacher approached coverage of uses of materials at Key Stage 1. It is an example of using formative assessment.

When analysing the work she intended to cover the teacher identified key vocabulary, concepts and skills that the children needed. She recognised that in this area of work it is important that children know the difference between an object and the material from which it is made. It is not the intention of this book to suggest that teachers should involve themselves in exhaustive testing before any teaching takes place. This would be counter-productive and waste valuable time. However, the teacher carried out a quick revision assessment in order to ensure that the children gained the maximum benefit from the work in hand. She used a simple table to gain valuable evidence on which to base decisions about the best teaching approach:

Object	Material it is made from

To reinforce the point and assess present levels of understanding the teacher asked the question in a slightly different way. The table below asks children to name three objects made from a selection of materials.

I want to know	I might be able to find out by
How many ants there are in a nest	Looking it up in a book
What snails like to eat	Giving them different foods to choose from
How many legs a caterpillar has	Looking at one through a lens or finding pictures of them

After clarifying any issues arising from this introductory work and identifying those children who needed some remedial help with basic concepts the teacher moved on to the main objective: why do we use a variety of materials for specific uses? The children had a number of actual objects to look at, handle and discuss and then use similar ways to record their ideas. Examination of the children's answers gave clear information to the teacher about how well the children understood the lesson about the use of materials. In addition the level of the answers gave a clear indication about the success of the teaching approach.

Object	Material it is made from	Why was that material chosen?

Formative assessment strategies

There are many useful strategies for carrying out formative assessment in primary science. In addition to being useful for assessment purposes many of these techniques can be used to vary the style of recording that children are asked to carry out. Assessment techniques include:

For more on learning objectives, see page 53, Chapter 6

1. modelling;
2. drawing explanatory diagrams and pictures;
3. labelling diagrams;
4. talking about cartoons and pictures;
5. simple structured tests;
6. word association;
7. more complex concept maps;
8. hot pen writing;
9. practical skills tests;
10. observing investigative work;
11. children's self-assessments.

Modelling

Modelling done by children can give their teachers an impression of their level of understanding. For instance, children given a lump of plasticine can use it to show their idea of the shape of the earth.

Drawing explanatory diagrams and pictures

Drawing explanatory diagrams and pictures can be a highly effective way to assess children's understanding. For instance, children can draw a picture of what they think happens to the sun at night. If the task is set with only a little guidance about the style and content of the drawing, the way in which the child represents what happens to the sun at night gives useful information about how to teach the child. For instance, a child who shows through his drawings that he thinks the sun goes behind the clouds, hills or mountains at the end of the day needs quite different teaching to the child who appreciates that the spinning of the earth causes the apparent motion of the sun. It is important to present tasks like this as fun – with a genuine and stated interest in finding out what the children already think.

At night the sun goes
behind the mountains.

Figure 8.1 Nine year old's drawing of the sun behind mountains

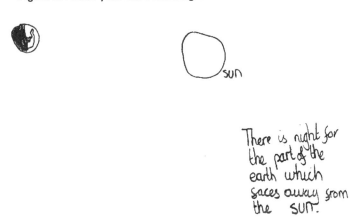

sun

There is night for
the part of the
earth which
faces away from
the sun.

Figure 8.2 Drawing of the earth and sun in orbit, by a nine-year-old child

In other contexts Key Stage 1 children can be asked to draw a number of sound sources, while Key Stage 2 children can be asked draw how they think sound reaches their ears. This style of assessment is very effective for delving into children's conceptual understanding and is likely to yield useful information about how to proceed.

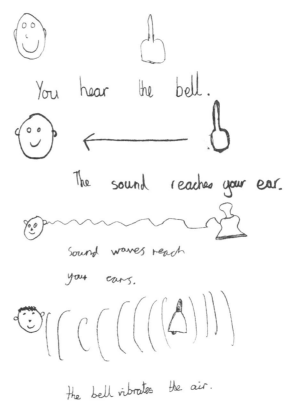

You hear the bell.

The sound reaches your ear.

Sound waves reach
your ears.

the bell vibrates the air.

Figure 8.3 Four possible ways in which sound reaches our ears. The first drawing is by a six-year-old child, the middle drawings by eight year olds and the last drawing is by a nine year old.

Labelling diagrams

Completing partly drawn diagrams and drawings can be a useful and efficient way of assessing what children know. In this instance the child has to add labels to the drawing of a plant. This mode of assessment is highly efficient in discovering a child's level of factual knowledge. Another context in which this might be used could involve the child being asked to show in a partially completed drawing how the light from a lamp helps a person to see an object which also figures in the drawing.

Talking about concept cartoons and pictures

For more on children's scientific ideas, see Chapter 2, and page 56, Chapter 6

Talking about concept cartoons and pictures is a fruitful way for children to begin to debate their ideas. This style of assessment encourages children to see that science can be a matter of opinion and that evidence is needed to support ideas. In a relaxed classroom children are likely to voice their ideas about what they think is likely to happen, and the listening teacher, while she may not gather a huge amount of information about an individual child, will gain a clearer understanding of the ideas of the class as a whole. There is a rich source of such material in Naylor and Keogh (2000). For instance, one of the many concept cartoons shows several children gathered around a snowman debating how best to keep him frozen.

What do YOU think?

Figure 8.4 An example of a concept cartoon

One child asserts that he will be best in a coat. Children reading the concept cartoon can be encouraged to join in the debate. There is no set right answer (as whether or not a coat will help depends on the air temperature and amount of sun) but the ideas offered by the children will give their teacher useful information about the correct level of work about melting and freezing.

Simple structured tests

Simple structured tests using pencil and paper are a useful source of assessment information. At the start of a unit of work in science many schools give their children a simple structured test. The tests help clarify what the children already know and what they need to know. The essence of a test like this is that it must be easy to administer and mark. If the child does the marking and he or she does the same or a similar test at the end of the period of study, they are likely to appreciate how much they have learnt.

Below is the outline of a test that might be useful to a Year 2 or Year 3 teacher about to start on some work about electricity. (In this test the diagrams have been replaced by brief descriptions due to lack of space.)

For more on starting with children's ideas, see page 39, Chapter 5

To devise these tests the teacher has looked at the level description for Attainment Target 4: physical processes (DfEE, 1999) to get the right level. Commercial test banks such as Peacock et al. (1998) offer a range of starting points for teachers to use when devising their own.

Question	Drawing	Level of the question and comments
What will happen when Tom turns on the switch?	Drawing of simple circuit with a switch.	Level 1: Change results from action.
What will happen when Jane switches on the torch?	Drawing of torch.	Level 1: Change results from action.
Which bulb will be brightest?	Simple torch bulb circuit and table lamp.	Level 2: Compare devices in electrical circuits.
Which of these bulbs will glow brightest?	Drawing of two circuits with bulbs, one with two batteries and identical one with only one battery.	Level 2: Compare devices in electrical circuits.
Why do you think that motor A will turn faster than motor B?	Drawing of two circuits with motors, one with two batteries and identical one with only one battery.	Level 3: Cause and effect.
Which of these bulbs will not glow? Explain your idea.	Drawing of two circuits with bulbs, one with a break in the circuit and the other complete.	Level 3: Link cause and effect in simple explanations.
Finish off this sentence to show what you know about electricity: If there are a lot of batteries in a circuit...	No drawing.	Level 3: beginning to make generalisations about physical phenomena.

Word association

Word association is the simple precursor to the use of concept maps. These allow children to record what they know rather than be reminded about what they don't know. Word association and concept maps ask children (and adults) to draw up a plan showing how they link different areas of knowledge. It makes concrete the connections we make between apparently disparate aspects of understanding. There are several levels to using concept maps with word association being the most basic. Write the word 'animal' – what do you associate with that word?

animal – dog

animal – cat

animal – boy

More complex concept maps

More complex concept maps involve asking children how they connect a wider range of words. Young children or lower-attaining older children can be given pictures and large arrows to arrange on the floor or a large table. For example, give a few large words already written – earth, sun, moon, orbit, star, planet and a selection of arrows. The children can arrange these on the floor and talk about the connections they are making. They can indicate connections by writing connecting words or sentences along the arrows.

Giving the children several words already written on a piece of paper along with small pieces of paper with words which the children might connect to the word on the larger sheet is a development from the pictures and large arrows. For instance, in QCA (1997) the words plant, pine tree and cactus are written on a sheet of paper and the following words are written on small pieces of paper:

hot, dry habitat
cold, snowy habitat
trunk
leaves
stem
spiky
thick

The children are invited to stick the words onto the page and then draw arrows connecting the words. The arrows can be labelled to indicate the way in which they are connected. For instance:

For more able or older children two main words, e.g. moon and earth, can be written on the board. As a class other words can be discussed which might be associated with the two main words. List these down the side: planet, star, orbit, seasons, day, night, spin, turn, eclipse, month, day, year, tilt, axis. Invite the children to construct their own concept diagrams before and after a Unit on the earth

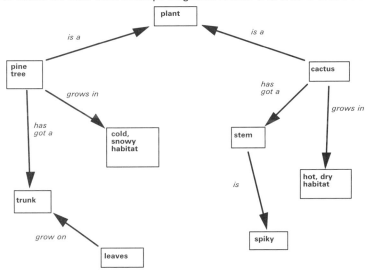

Figure 8.5 A concept map

and beyond. Allow more able children more freedom by omitting the list of words and invite them to link words of their own.

> **RESEARCH SUMMARY** RESEARCH SUMMARY **RESEARCH SUMMARY**
>
> Kitchin (2000) researched the use teachers make of concept maps. He mainly looked at secondary students but his detailed analysis is highly relevant for all primary school teachers. Kitchin discusses the importance of allowing children to own their maps and for teachers not to become obsessed with the correctness of the map. Kitchin suggests that focusing on the correctness of a map turns the process into transmission teaching but acknowledges that the idiosyncratic maps produced by pupils are difficult for teachers to interpret.
>
> Kitchin suggests that maps tend to fall into three pattern categories:
>
> - **Spoke – which Kitchin suggests represents the National Curriculum structure;**
> - **Chain – which Kitchin suggests represents a non-integrated lesson sequence;**
> - **Net – which Kitchin suggests represents meaningful learning.**
>
> The author goes on to analyse the finer details of concept maps, looking in particular at the quality of the links between concepts. The strain of scoring and assessing the maps in quantitative ways is discussed in the paper. Two examples of concept maps flowing from the word 'flower' are used to illustrate the idea that children will produce quite different and idiosyncratic maps if they have different overall ideas. In the cases quoted one of the children constructed a map based on plant reproduction while another child produced a map concerned mainly with the interaction of flowers with insects.

Hot pen writing

Hot pen writing is usually much enjoyed by children. Invite them to write and draw all they know about the topic you are about to begin. Give them a very tight time schedule such as ten minutes. Again, after studying the topic, ask the children to repeat the exercise and compare the two versions. This provides invaluable information for evaluative assessment.

Practical skills tests

Activities that test skills can give very clear indications of children's abilities in the area of scientific enquiry. For instance, before the class carries out an investigation into the rate of cooling of water in different containers, it may be useful to assess whether the children can read the types of thermometers you have in the classroom. If the vast majority can already do so then moments have been wasted, but if many children are still unsure then revision of reading scales would be productive. One extremely simple way to test this skill is to hand out thermometers to the children as they leave the classroom and ask them to whisper the reading into the teacher's ear as they go out to break.

Observing investigative work

Assessing classroom work is a routine part of the teacher's role. How teachers respond to children's work makes important differences to the way that children perceive their achievement. Many children feel that teachers judge neatness, spelling and punctuation rather than content. It is relatively easy to home in on these features as they are relatively easy to assess compared with aspects of content which may require longer comments. Perhaps we should aim for quality of comment rather than frequency.

The comments written by teachers on children's work can have important effects. Black and Wiliam (1998) note, not surprisingly, that children generally dislike negative comments. However, while positive comments are welcomed by children, they find that simple comments like 'Good' are of little use to them. Children want to know what they can do to improve the content of their work and not simply their presentation. Comments should set targets for children. Teachers who set simple attainable targets for children in the context of comments on work encourage children to believe they can gain greater success in their work. Given achievable yet challenging targets they can become children who are motivated by a desire to learn rather than a desire to be seen to do well. Comments that contain targets are likely to lead children to believe they can improve. These might include:

'I liked the way you wrote about your results – can you explain a little more about what you did?'

'Your graph was easy to read – can you make the title describe more accurately what the graph is about?'

'The labelled drawing of your flower had four labels on it. Can you add two more?'

The judgements made about children's work should, as often as possible, be ipsative, i.e. the work should always be compared with the standard that the individual produced previously rather than being compared to the class as a whole. The latter may lead to the less able becoming disheartened and the able children becoming complacent.

REFLECTIVE TASK

Read the book by De Boo, *Enquiring Children, Challenging Teaching* (1999), and use the suggestions for assessment at the end of each chapter. The suggestions offered in the book are not focused exclusively on the National Curriculum and are all the better for it. Take, for instance, a couple of the suggestions from p. 51 for assessing young children investigating the environment:

- **Are the children interested and involved throughout the activity?**
- **Do the children show confidence when faced with unexpected results?**
- **Do the children cooperate with others during the investigation?**

Devise some similar assessment questions of your own, linked to learning objectives, to use informally to help judge the progress of individuals or the success of a session.

Children's self-assessment

Children's own assessment has a key role in the development of the child as a learner. Black (1998) sees that one of the main reasons for children to be intimately involved in the assessment of their own learning is that they will shoulder more of the responsibility for their own learning if they are involved in assessing their own progress. Black (1998) discusses how, at the present time, many children see the results of any assessment as summative rather than formative. When we consider the single comment 'Good' (see 'Observing investigative work' above) this is obviously a summative comment – it has little or no formative content. Similarly, 'You could try harder' is perceived as summative by most children, especially those who have tried as hard as they possibly can already.

In order to assess their own progress, children need information about what they are learning. In particular they need to know the objective for a particular session and also the context in which the learning takes place. So, for instance, it is useful to know the objective for a particular lesson, e.g. 'We are going to learn the names of the parts of the flower'. Or even more helpfully perhaps: 'Flowers are the way in which some plants make seeds so we are going to see which parts are involved in doing that and give them names.'

One strategy that may help children's self-assessment is to ask the children what they would like to know about the topic they are about to study and how they might do this. For example they could draw up a simple table:

I want to know	I might be able to find out by
How many ants there are in a nest	Looking it up in a book
What snails like to eat	Giving them different foods to choose from
How many legs a caterpillar has	Looking at one through a lens or finding pictures of them

- **Give the children small attainable targets to aim for in their learning and ask them how far they feel they have met them.**
- **Tell the children about the learning objective for the session.**
- **Emphasise the learning that children have achieved rather than the things they do not know by using assessment strategies such as concept maps (see above).**
- **After the learning ask children to list what they have learnt and to compare their concept maps from the beginning of the work with those from the end.**
- **Help children to see where their learning fits into the bigger picture.**
- **Involve the children in assessing each other's work.**

Recording formative assessment

Recording formative assessments must involve as little work as possible for the teacher. A simple grid such as the one below will suffice for most everyday purposes. Avoid rewriting the children's names each time by compiling a simple mark book.

	Objective: to be able to distinguish magnetic from non-magnetic materials 20/9/06	Objective: to draw up a table showing magnetic and non-magnetic materials 23/9/06	Objective: to be able to design a test to test relative strength of three magnets 27/9/06	Objective:
James Brown	1 a	2 a	2 b	
Karen Gee	1 c	1 b	1 c	
Ahmed Khan	1 a	1 a	3 b	
etc.				

Key
Level of ipsative achievement (i.e. how did they do relative to their usual standard?)
1 = high   2 = average   3 = poor

Level of criterion-referenced achievement (i.e. did they achieve objective?)
a = high   b = average   c = poor

In addition to this everyday record, teachers may keep slim files of some assessed work to compare standards with other teachers. They would also find it helpful to refer to a summative record of each child in the class. A record such as the one below helps in several ways.

- **It is easy to compile using information from the everyday record.**
- **It indicates which children are making rapid or slow progress relative to the class as a whole.**
- **It indicates the level of the majority of the class.**

	Level 1				Level 2				Level 3				Level 4				Level 5			
	AT 1	AT 2	AT 3	AT 4	AT 1	AT 2	AT 3	AT 4	AT 1	AT 2	AT 3	AT 4	AT 1	AT 2	AT 3	AT 4	AT 1	AT 2	AT 3	AT 4
James Brown	x	x	x	x	x	/	/	/	/											
Karen Gee	x	x	x	x	x	x	x	x	/	/	x	/								
Ahmed Khan	x	x	x	x	x	x	x	x	x	x	x	x	x	x	x	/				
etc.																				

Key: A line to show some understanding and a cross to show mastery of content. In the actual document a summary of the content is shown. In this extract Ahmed is assessed as having achieved all of level 3 and is near to achieving level 4. (See more complete table in Peacock et al., 1997.)

Reporting

Reports to parents should contain as much information in as straightforward a style as possible. Some schools only employ longhand reports while others use tick sheets which can convey a great deal of information very efficiently. Read this report which is based on the child 'David' whose work can be seen in SCAA (1995).

> *David is an observant boy who is keen to discuss his ideas with others. He enjoys science and puts forward his own ideas and suggestions about why things happen. He is methodical in his written work and conveys his ideas clearly. He can use diagrammatic symbols for electrical components and he labels diagrams with care. He records his findings in tables where appropriate. He links cause and effect in many of his explanations which can sometimes be full and give a clear picture of what he has done. On occasions David is able to make generalisations from his work but he needs help to make connections between related phenomena and he needs assistance to interpret his results correctly. There are occasions when David gives partial explanations in his work and he sometimes misses out important details. David makes interesting links between things he has noticed in the environment and his work in science. Overall David's work is satisfactory for this class but slightly below average for his year group nationally.*

Read the report and consider the following.

- **Is the last sentence true?**
- **Is it useful?**
- **Will the child be disheartened?**
- **Does it imply the class is below national standards?**
- **Would the parents be pleased if the writer had been less blunt?**

Do you think it is possible to design a tick sheet which can convey all this information more efficiently?

Summative assessment

National tests are compulsory in science at Y6 and optional at Y2. An assessment unit for Y4 was introduced in 1997 (QCA, 1997). Tests like this may be used to demonstrate how much children have progressed relative to the previous year. The national tests are criterion-referenced in that all children who answer to a set standard for a particular level can be awarded that level irrespective of the number of others who achieve the same standard.

Summative judgements are made by teachers at several points in the school year, most notably in compiling end-of-year reports. However, the highest status and highest stakes summative judgements are undoubtedly the end of key stage SATs. These tests may have their place in evaluating the effectiveness of different schools but they are a poor model for formative assessments in that they:

- **give a single number summarising a range of data;**
- **provide very little in the way of detail for future work;**
- **insist on one style of collecting data;**
- **must have a clear paper evidence trail against which to judge the findings.**

RESEARCH SUMMARY RESEARCH SUMMARY **RESEARCH SUMMARY**

There is a considerable body of literature concerning the progression of children from one key stage to the next. Peacock and Smith (1999) report that there is considerable evidence to suggest that teachers in subsequent key stages distrust the judgements made by teachers in the key stage below. This is particularly marked in Key Stage 3 where teachers typically take little notice of the assessments made by teachers in Key Stage 2. Bunyan (1998) reported a study comparing child performance in Key Stages 2 and 3 national tests in science in which he found that it is no more easy to obtain a level 5 in the Key Stage 2 paper than it is in the Key Stage 3 paper. In fact, his results indicated that the opposite may be true.

A SUMMARY OF **KEY POINTS**

> **Formative assessment helps teachers plan the next step for their children.**

> **Assessment provides teachers with information about their own effectiveness.**

> **Assessment can frequently take place in the context of everyday classroom activities.**

> **There is a range of available strategies for formative assessment.**

> **Children value feedback from their teachers that helps them to make progress.**

> **Record-keeping need not be overly time-consuming.**

> **Reports to parents need to be honest and encouraging.**

Moving on

Focus in your NQT year on using assessment for learning. Look for opportunities to informally assess pupils then tailor your interventions appropriately. For instance, quickly ask individuals to sketch their ideas showing how a periscope might work. Teach in a way which acknowledges what the children think already.

FURTHER READING   FURTHER READING   **FURTHER READING**

Arthur, J. et al. (2006) *Learning to Teach in the Primary School*. Abingdon: Routledge.

Black, P. (1998) *Testing: Friend or Foe?* Brighton: Falmer. The authoritative source of information about assessment.

Overall, L. and Sangster, M. (2006) *Assessment: A Practical Guide for Primary Teachers*. London: Continuum.

Naylor, S. and Keogh, B. (2004) *Active Assessment*. London: Fulton.

REFERENCES REFERENCES **REFERENCES** REFERENCES REFERENCES

Black, P. (1998) *Testing: Friend or Foe?* Brighton: Falmer.

Black, P. and Wiliam, D. (1998) 'Assessment and classroom learning', *Assessment in Education*, 5(1), 7–74.

Bunyan, P. (1998) 'Comparing pupil performance in Key Stages 2 and 3 Science SATs', *School Science Review*, 79(289), 85–8.

De Boo, M. (1999) *Enquiring Children, Challenging Teaching*. Buckingham: Open University Press.

DfES (2007) *http://www.standards.dfes.gov.uk.ts/*

Kitchin, I. (2000) 'Using concept maps to reveal understanding: a two tier analysis', *School Science Review*, 81(296), 41–6.

Naylor, S. and Keogh, B. (2000) *Concept Cartoons in Science Education*. Cheshire: Millgate House.

Peacock, G. and Smith, R. (1999) *Do Children Repeat Science from One Key Stage to the Next?*, in Proceedings of the 4th Summer Conference for Teacher Education in Primary Science, University of Durham.

Peacock, G., Jesson J. and Ridgeway, H. (1998) *Sciencecheck*. London: Collins Educational.

Peacock, G. et al. (1997) *Science Connections*. Harlow: Longman.

QCA (1997) *Year 4 Assessment, Unit 2*. London: QCA.

SCAA (1995) *Exemplification of Standards: Science*. London: SCAA.

9
Using ICT in science

Introduction

What counts as ICT (Information and Communications Technology)? QCA (1998, p. 19) defines it as: *The computing and communications facilities and features that variously support teaching, learning and a range of activities in education*. The same document goes on to say that Information Technology (IT) comprises the knowledge and skills needed to use ICT. Not all IT involves computers, but most does. Some IT might be a preparation for computer use, as is the case when using paper and pencil to help understand how binary databases work before using the computer, or using a thermometer before using a computer sensor. In this chapter we concentrate on the use of computers in the classroom, with only a few remarks

For more on the best way to organise computer use, see page 75, Chapter 7

about other important aspects of ICT such as the telephone, video, radio and tape recorder.

Using ICT to teach science is not an end in itself. The use of computers should always enhance the learning of science and not focus on the technology itself. Teachers should consider whether using the computer for a particular task really assists learning in science. If it does not, then the same task should be done in another way.

The main uses of a computer in science are:

- *Writing reports* and descriptions mainly using word processing and incorporating spreadsheets, photos and drawings;
- *Storing and manipulating information* mainly using spreadsheets and databases;
- *Using sensors* to detect changes in the environment in the context of computer datalogging;
- *Obtaining information* from electronic sources such as web sites and CD ROMs;
- *Imaging* when using digital camera or scanner linked to a computer;
- *Drawing* using drawing programs;
- *Communicating* through email and networks;
- *Teachers' own use of ICT* in their planning.

Writing reports and descriptions

For more on presentations, see page 45, Chapter 5

Always consider whether using the computer keyboard to get children to record the results of their work in science is worthwhile. What are the advantages and disadvantages?

Advantages of ICT	Disadvantages of ICT
Reports on investigative work can be worthwhile because when using a word processor, children can create first drafts at the computer either individually or collaboratively and then edit the work without tedious rewriting.	It ties the computer up for hours at a time.
Children like using the computer.	There is usually time spent getting the computer to work correctly, or teaching the children ICT skills as opposed to science.
The finished work looks more polished. Spellcheckers and tools can assist the children to focus on the science and not the recording.	Children and teachers can get obsessed with getting every full stop and comma correct before the work is pronounced finished. The work done at the computer can, unwittingly and unjustifiably, be given more recognition than writing using pen and paper.
The files of previous work can be saved very efficiently.	There can be a great deal of frustration when a hard disk crashes or material is inadvertently wiped.

Many teachers use simple proformas to help children plan for their science investigation. For Key Stage 1 children an example may go along the lines:

Our question
What we are going to do
What we think might happen.

These three entries can be saved by the teacher as a *template* and added to by groups of children. The rest of the report can be added to the first part later.

What happened?
Our explanation.

RESEARCH SUMMARY RESEARCH SUMMARY **RESEARCH SUMMARY**

In some senses this is not research but the distillation of experience from a teacher about the use of word processors in science teaching. In his article Tebbutt (1997) offers a comprehensive review of the way in which word processing can be used in science teaching. He discusses the use of word processors to:

- **produce worksheets;**
- **allow free writing and recording;**
- **help with guided writing including cloze exercises, sequencing and word searches;**
- **help children plan experiments.**

Storing and manipulating information

A spreadsheet is a matrix of cells that you can use as a table of results. Once it has been filled in you can sort the results, carry out calculations and quickly draw a variety of graphs. This then allows time for the interpretation of the graph rather than spending time on the mechanics of drawing. Microsoft's Excel is a sophisticated spreadsheet for use on the PC. At first glance Excel might seem to be inappropriate for Key Stage 1 children but it can easily be tailored to meet their needs by changing the font size, the width of the cells and the colour of the data entry. Teachers can easily set up an empty bar chart which fills as children enter their data. Frost (1995) has a wide range of suggestions for using spreadsheets.

So why use spreadsheets? The touchstone always has to be whether using the computer helps children learn the science. In the case of spreadsheets there are three main benefits:

- **the speed and ease of drawing graphs and charts – pie charts, for instance, are easy to interpret but difficult to draw without a computer;**
- **the speed and ease of calculating outcomes (e.g. averages) – especially if the teacher has devised a template, it is easy for children to enter data and have the computer automatically calculate the outcome;**
- **the simplicity of entering data into a prepared table that can be saved, altered and easily compared with others.**

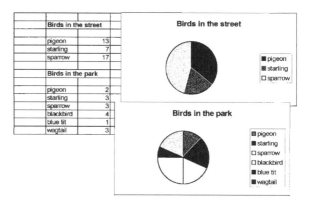

Figure 9. 1 What can you learn from these charts? What would children learn?

Using databases to collate and sort information has several applications in primary science. It is usually easier to draw graphs using a spreadsheet. However, the branching databases (or dichotomous databases) are important as an extension from sorting and classifying materials and objects. It leads logically on to children constructing their own keys. The instructions on the computer guide users through the process of using the branching database, but is also desirable for children to draw out the structure of the key on paper. A branching database for small animals might look something like this:

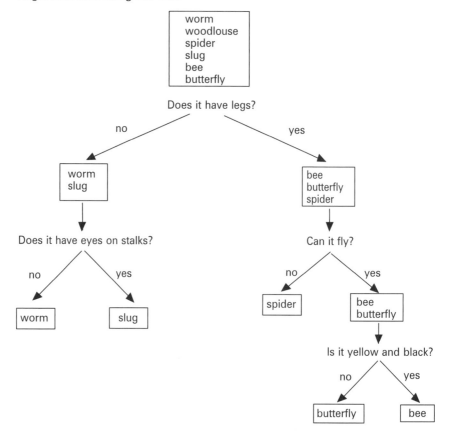

Figure 9.2 A branching database for small animals

Databases such as Microsoft Access and Junior Pinpoint are relatively complex to use and are rarely of much utility in primary science since usually there are not sufficiently large quantities of information to manipulate. However, a large school-wide database that incorporates all the invertebrate animals and plants in the school grounds, for instance, could be useful if it is added to over the years.

So why use databases?

- **It is easier to add items to a computer database than it is to add to a paper database. Information can be collated and displayed in a number of ways. The computer can very swiftly identify items requested by the user.**

Using sensors

Datalogging simply involves plugging sensors, which record temperature, light, sound or movement, into a small box attached to the computer. You then run a program that records the readings on the sensors. These readings are then plotted on a graph. The fact that a graph is built up in real time is a very useful teaching tool. Several manufacturers produce datalogging equipment, the most popular being produced by LogIT and Philip Harris.

Some dataloggers have to be plugged into the computer that records the readings of the sensors. Equipment of this type includes LogIT Live. Other datalogging equipment can be used away from the computer, allowing the data to be uploaded

For a practical example of the outdoor use of this approach, see page 105

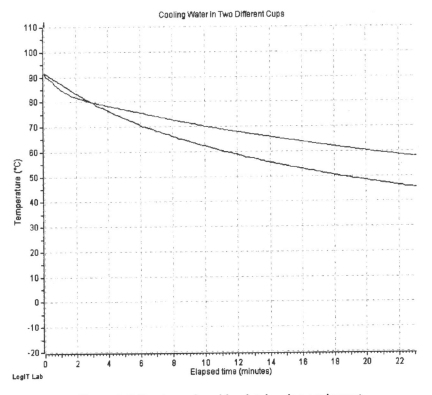

Figure 9. 3 Graph produced by datalogging equipment

to the computer at a later stage. LogIT can be used away from the computer and can record many readings for later use. The change in air temperature outside over a 24-hour period compared with the changes in pond water temperature and the temperature under a large stone in the same period can lead to discussion about why some habitats are more productive than others.

Here are some of the possible areas of use for datalogging equipment:

Light

- **Which sunglasses let most light through?**
- **Which fabric is best for curtains?**
- **What happens to the light readings as you move the sensor further away from a torch?**
- **Which source of light is brightest?**
- **Which road safety reflective strip reflects most light?**

For more on asking questions, see page 60, Chapter 6

Sound

- **Make a sound plot of the room you are in. Write a sound story to explain the graph.**
- **Which material makes the best sound insulator?**
- **What happens to sound level as you move away from/towards a sound source?**

Temperature

- **Which insulation material slows cooling best?**
- **Do large volumes of water cool more slowly than small ones? How does this relate to large and small animals in the Arctic?**
- **What happens to the temperature of icy water left in the classroom?**
- **What happens to the temperature in the classroom on a sunny day?**

So why use a computer to measure light, sound and temperature when there are manual methods of doing this? The computer produces a table of results instantly and converts them into a graph very easily. The children can then get on with interpreting the graph rather than spending a long time turning laboriously collected data into a graph. For instance, in an experiment where children compare the insulation properties of different materials more of the limited time available in the classroom can be devoted to interpreting the graph rather than collecting the information and then turning it into a graph.

Obtaining information

Books are likely to remain the most efficient way of collecting information for some time to come. However, electronic sources of information can be a very useful addition.

For more on primary and secondary sources, see page 43, Chapter 5

CD-ROMs (compact disc read-only memory) contain a huge amount of data on a single disc. They are surprisingly inexpensive and can support a range of work in science. Interactive programs such as Two-Can's *Polar Lands* and *Electricity and Magnetism* are good ways to extend practical work. In the excellent *Electricity and Magnetism*, for instance, children can make circuits at the click of a mouse and see what happens when they make parallel and series circuits. They can easily see the effects of switches and resistors. It's no substitute for handling the real thing but a superb addition to the children's range of experience.

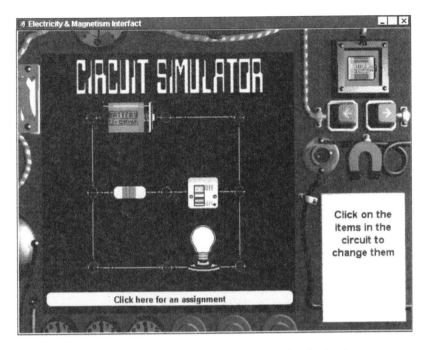

For more on ways of giving instructions, see page 43, Chapter 5

For more on planning to teach electricity, see page 56, Chapter 6

Figure 9.4 Electricity and magnetism circuit simulator

RESEARCH SUMMARY RESEARCH SUMMARY RESEARCH SUMMARY

Wellington (1999) writing about using multimedia with secondary students reports on the results from a large-scale trial which utilised multimedia presentations to help children understand chemical processes. In this survey there was no data from primary schools but results from the two phases are likely to be similar.

The study reported the advantages of using multimedia computer programs. They:
- **made the invisible processes visible;**
- **allowed dynamic images (unlike books);**
- **had an attractive visual impact;**
- **gave enrichment to the more able and supported the less able;**
- **allowed easy and fruitful repetition.**

There were clear problems using multimedia programs:
- **Children play with the programs rather than learn the content.**
- **There is too much information.**
- **There are annoying levels of noise from the program.**
- **Groups not using the computer can cause a distraction.**
- **They might possibly replace real-life experience.**

NB: To help set this research into a primary context consider the way in which children use programs such as those in the Two-Can Interface range (e.g. *Electricity and Magnetism* – Page, 1997) and those produced by Dorling Kindersley (e.g. *The Way Things Work*).

The *internet* is changing the way information is gathered. One major problem is knowing how to get the information you require. You may know the address of the information source you are seeking; for example, *http://www.nhm.ac.uk* will take you to the excellent site of the Natural History Museum. Teachers and children can search the web for information on specific science subjects using a variety of search engines such as Lycos, HotBot, InfoSeek and Excite. Each search engine has its idiosyncrasies and there is on-line help.

PRACTICAL TASK PRACTICAL TASK PRACTICAL TASK PRACTICAL TASK

To look for information on pinhole cameras try Google and type in +pinhole +camera. (The plus signs means that these words must be included in any search results.)

In QCA (1998) it is suggested that children are taught about the changes in the length of the day during the year. For detailed information on sunrise and sunset times go to altavista.com and type +sunset +UK

Use the web to find something related to your current planning for science.

So why use the internet when there are books around? Try doing the last task in any other way. This author found it very difficult to obtain such comprehensive information through any other source.

Imaging

Digital cameras and scanners are extremely useful devices for use in primary science. Digital cameras make the results of photography immediately accessible by children and easily incorporated into their written work. Uses for digital cameras include:

- recording a tree from season to season;
- photographing parts of the school grounds to incorporate in reports e-mailed to classes in other parts of the country or even across the world;
- recording what the children did at different stages of an experiment.

Uses for scanners include:

- scanning copyright-free images into the children's work;
- scanning the detailed structure of a leaf or flower (care should taken not to scratch the glass);
- scanning in text from a book for the children to manipulate as part of their work.

So why use a digital camera when there are ordinary Polaroid cameras? Digital cameras are easy to use and the results are almost instant. Images can be saved and pasted into any number of documents very quickly and at little expense. The resulting photographs can be sent to schools in different parts of the world via e-mail. The use of video web cams will make this style of communicating even more exciting and immediate.

Drawing

Drawing and paint programs on computers have relatively little application in science. However, it is relatively easy for children to use drawing programs to draw electrical symbols that can then be duplicated, moved around and pasted into new circuit diagrams.

Communicating

The ease and speed of e-mail communication means that it is possible for children in a class in Birmingham to communicate with a similar class in Penzance or Perth, Australia. E-mails can carry attachments including photographs, documents and graphs. This is especially useful when communicating the results of experiments, weather conditions or reports on the environment of the school grounds. The results of plant growth experiments in Aberdeen, London and Sydney in January would be quite different and useful comparisons could be made. Climatic information and information about observations of the sun and moon can be sent quickly and easily from other continents.

So why use the internet? The immediacy of the information from school to school promotes learning through collaboration and discussion.

Teachers' own use of ICT

The range of information available to teachers to help plan their own teaching is large. Use the National Grid for Learning at *ngfl.gov.uk*, for instance, to get information about museums and other sources of information to help plan lessons and visits.

IN THE CLASSROOM

Using ICT to teach Y4 children about habitats

In this project the teacher used a range of techniques to help her class study the school grounds. She used ICT where she felt it was appropriate. In this account the use of ICT is highlighted but it was only one of the ways in which the children learnt about the local animals and plants.

Looking at different habitats

The teacher explained to the children that a habitat was the place where an animal or plant lived. She told them to look at their school grounds for a range of habitats. They used maps and plans to mark down the locations of the different habitats they found. They used a digital camera at each location to record what each habitat looked like. The teacher felt that the use of the digital camera was justified because it would record quickly and easily the habitats in a way that no other medium would (except a standard camera, but that would take time to develop).

In the class the children worked in groups at a word processor to write about two of the habitats they had seen. They incorporated the digital camera images into their writing. This was in addition to drawings done by the children, which were also added to the written accounts.

For more on grouping and computers, see page 67, Chapter 7

Common minibeasts

The teacher realised that the children would be particularly interested in the minibeasts they found in the different habitats. To start the project with a high level of interest she and the children went on a minibeast hunt. At first they were only interested in finding a range of such creatures and looking at their features rather than a detailed survey of where they were found. In this way they found slugs, snails, earwigs, woodlice, aphids, shield bugs, worms, beetles (including ladybirds) and centipedes. The children identified the animals using a range of references including paper and electronic sources. The children scanned in pictures of several of the minibeasts adding labels and a caption to each one. The teacher felt that this activity was a good use of ICT because the children were actively using the high quality scanned diagrams after identifying and finding out about the animals at first hand.

For more on scanning, see page 102

Using computers to sort

Initially the teacher started by playing 20 questions orally about a variety of topics including minibeasts. (**Teacher**: I'm thinking of a minibeast. **Children**: Does it have legs? **Teacher**: Yes. **Children**: Does it...) The children then sorted the minibeasts that they and the teacher had found using a computer branching database. In the classroom the teacher used the wall map of the school to remind the children about the different habitats they had identified. She asked the children where they expected to find particular animals and asked them to make predictions based on what they had found out about the animals. For example, 'I expect to find aphids on roses and sycamore trees because they suck sap'; 'I expect we will find worms in the soil because they burrow'. She then assigned different groups of children to look for animals in two different habitats. Each group had to record the number of each kind of minibeast they found in each location.

For more on using branching databases, see page 98

Combining information

The teacher wanted the children to pool their numerical data on the different habitats so they could check their predictions. She designed a spreadsheet which showed the names of the habitats across the top and the names of the animals down the side. The groups took it in turns to enter the numbers for their habitats. She felt that the use of the computer spreadsheet was justified here because the data would be available to all groups in a variety of different forms. She felt it could be manipulated and added to in a way that paper records could not be.

The teacher felt that the whole chart was a useful resource but that it was too difficult for most of the children to interpret. Indeed, when she made a bar chart from the data it was interesting for the highest ability children who loved the 3D bars. However, she showed the children how to highlight a selection of the spreadsheet to produce a much simpler chart. Before any charts were produced the teacher insisted that the children tell her what they wanted the data to show. The teacher felt the speed at which each group could produce graphs and charts to support or reject a prediction made using the computer worthwhile.

For more on spreadsheets, see page 97

Number of each minibeast in each habitat				
	Under the stone	In the short grass	In the long grass	In the flowerbed
spider	1	0	1	1
worm	3	0	0	3
slug	4	0	1	0
snail	1	0	1	1
woodlice	5	0	0	2

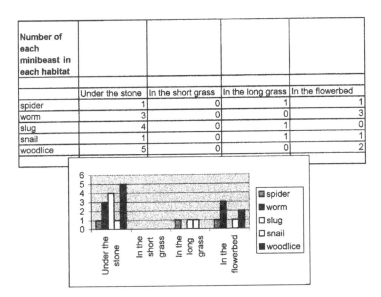

Figure 9.5 Bar chart produced from data

Using a datalogger

The teacher asked the children why some environments, e.g. under the carpet, under the stone and in the long grass, had so many types of animals while the school field and the soil at the base of a wall had few. She introduced the children to simple datalogging equipment. To show the children how it worked the teacher set up the datalogger to record changes in their own classroom habitat over a 24-hour period.

The children offered their ideas about why some habitats had such a diversity of animal life. Some of the ideas included the suggestion that some habitats did not dry out or heat up during the day as much as others. At first the children used their fingers to test humidity, thermometers to measure temperature and their eyes to estimate the amount of shade.

The teacher set up a datalogger (which did not need to be connected to a computer) in several different habitats over the course of a week, though she was restricted to daytime because of the chance of theft. She also set up a datalogger to take readings of light, temperature and moisture over the school day. (See the web site **http://www.vtc.ngfl.gov.uk/resource/cits/science/prfocus/psinvest/day1.html** for an example of this investigation.) Three contrasting habitats were measured in this way and the results compared.

For more on datalogging, see page 99

Communicating findings

The teacher had previously communicated with a teacher in another school where the children were also studying their school grounds. The children in the two schools communicated their findings to each other using e-mail attachments which included the word-processed information, spreadsheets, databases and photographs.

For more on e-mail, see page 103

A SUMMARY OF **KEY POINTS**

> Computers can be used in science education to do many tasks more quickly and easily than conventional methods.

> Graphs and charts can be drawn quickly and easily using spreadsheets and data-bases.

> Datalogging devices enable children to take a series of accurate readings over different periods of time and then quickly produce charts and graphs.

> CD-ROMs provide an alternative to conventional books. They provide motivation and flexibility in learning.

> The Internet can be used to provide information for teachers and children that might be difficult to find elsewhere.

Moving on

Computers and other communications devices will undoubtedly become cheaper and more powerful. Focus on a few selected uses of ICT and become really familiar with them in your NQT year. You might make frequent use of spreadsheets and branch keys, for instance, rather than trying to use the full range of possibilities.

FURTHER READING FURTHER READING **FURTHER READING**

Ager, R. (1998) *Information and Communications Technology in Primary Schools: Children or Computers in Control?* London: Fulton. A useful book which covers a range of issues about using computers in the classroom.

Harlen, W. (2004) *The Teaching of Science in Primary Schools*. London: Fulton.

Meadows, J. (2004) *Science and ICT in the Primary School: A Creative Approach to Big Ideas*. London: Fulton.

QCA (1998) *A Scheme of Work for Key Stages 1 and 2: Information Technology*. London: QCA. The pupils' National Curriculum requirements.

REFERENCES REFERENCES **REFERENCES** REFERENCES REFERENCES

Frost, R. (1995) *IT in Primary Science*. Hatfield: ASE.

Page, J. (1997) *Electricity and Magnetism* (Interact series). London: Two-Can.

QCA (1998) *A Scheme of Work for Key Stages 1 and 2: Science*. London: QCA.

Tebbutt, M. (1997) 'Word-processors in science teaching – why?', *School Science Review*, 79(287), 91–9.

Wellington, J. (1999) 'Integrating multimedia into science teaching', *School Science Review*, 81(295), 49–54.

10
Health and safety

Professional Standards for QTS

Those awarded QTS must have a secure knowledge and understanding of science that enables them to teach effectively across the age and ability for which they are trained. To be able to do this in the context of the nature of scientific understanding trainees should:

Professional attributes

Q3(a) Be aware of the professional duties of teachers and the statutory framework within which they work.

(b) Be aware of the policies and practices of the workplace and share in collective responsibility for their implementation.

Professional knowledge and understanding

Q21(a) Be aware of current legal requirements, national policies and guidance on the safeguarding and promotion of the well-being of children and young people.

(b) Know how to identify and support children and young people whose progress, development or well-being is affected by changes or difficulties in their personal circumstances, and when to refer them to colleagues for specialist support.

Professional skills

Q30 Establish a purposeful and safe learning environment conducive to learning and identify opportunities for learners to learn in and out of school contexts.

Q32 Work as a team member and identify opportunities for working with colleagues, sharing the development of effective practice with them.

Introduction

Primary schools are, as would be expected, relatively safe places to work. Under most normal circumstances, the wide variety of tasks undertaken in primary classrooms is generally not a source of danger to children and reported accidents or incidents as a result of primary science activity are rare. It is essential in the planning, teaching, organisation and management of primary science that relevant health and safety matters are taken into account in order to prevent avoidable injury and that all reasonable steps are taken to establish a safe and secure environment for everyone.

For more on planning, teaching strategies and organisation and management, see Chapters 5, 6 and 7

RESEARCH SUMMARY RESEARCH SUMMARY RESEARCH SUMMARY

Codes of conduct for health and safety in primary science are available in all school and local authority (LA) science policies. These should be followed rigorously. The Association for Science Education (ASE – http://www.ase.org.uk), the School Science Service (CLEAPSS – http://www.cleapss.org.uk) and the Scottish Schools Equipment Research Centre (SSERC – http://www.sserc.org.uk) also provide health and safety information for primary science. The ASE's publication *Be Safe!* and health and safety guides and newsletters from CLEAPSS are particularly useful and should be consulted as a matter of routine. Additional advice about keeping animals in schools can be obtained from the Royal Society for the Protection of Cruelty to Animals (RSPCA – http://www.rspca.org.uk). All schools and LAs issue codes of conduct for off-site visits. These should be followed rigorously. Further information about off-site visits can be obtained from the Department for Education and Skills (DfES – http://www.dfes.gov.uk).

Legal requirements

Teachers, including trainees and NQTs, have a common law duty to ensure that children are safe on school premises and during off-site visits. This is bestowed upon them by acting *in loco parentis* ('in the place of a parent'). When acting *in loco parentis*, teachers are generally expected to exercise more care than would normally be expected of a careful parent. All teachers, including trainees and NQTs, also have a duty to work in accordance with the Health and Safety at Work etc. Act 1974. The Health and Safety at Work etc. Act points out that employers, such as LAs and governing bodies, are required to keep schools as safe as is reasonably practicable and foreseeable for all who use or visit them. Sections 7 and 8 of the Act are more specific:

- **teachers have a statutory and contractual obligation to cooperate with their employers in all matters relating to health and safety;**
- **teachers must not only take reasonable care for the health and safety of themselves, they must also take reasonable care for the health and safety of others;**
- **teachers should not intentionally or recklessly interfere with or misuse anything provided in the interests of health and safety.**

Just as acting *in loco parentis* and the Health and Safety at Work etc. Act are important to schools as a whole, they also apply when teaching science. Enquiries about health and safety in any school should be directed to the appointed health and safety representative or, for primary science, to the science coordinator.

The language of health and safety includes hazards, risks, risk assessment and risk management:

- *hazards* – **result in exposure or vulnerability to injury, may be connected with the resources and methods used by teachers or children in teaching and learning science;**
- *risks* – **the perceived or actual likelihood of hazards resulting in injury, may be high or low depending on the nature of the hazards, the injury likely to be sustained, and the number of people likely to be involved;**
- *risk assessment* – **identifies all hazards and likely outcomes in advance of their happening, provides the basis for selecting safe ways to proceed;**

- *risk management* – identifies and adopts strategies to produce a zero risk level or at least minimise the potential for risk, ensures that all reasonable precautions are taken and codes of conduct followed.

At all times, teachers are advised to avoid any potential for allegations of negligence associated with work in science and never to assume that any activities that get into print are safe to do!

Safe science

Health and safety requirements vary according to the science being taught, the resources and methods used, the number of children involved, the level of supervision required, the physical layout of the classroom or teaching area, and so on. They can also vary from school to school and authority to authority. All teachers should be familiar with the layout of the school, where entrances and emergency exits are, the location of fire alarms and firefighting appliances, fire drills and other emergency procedures, and the siting of telephones, particularly if engaged in activities associated with running an after-school science club. The following pointers draw attention to some of the more common aspects of health and safety requiring careful attention.

Humans

- Avoid touching, tasting, handling or picking up foodstuffs unless it is absolutely safe to do so.
- Ensure meticulous care in choice, storage, preparation, use and disposal of foodstuffs.
- Avoid contamination of foodstuffs.
- Sterilise all utensils and work areas.
- Ensure meticulous attention to personal hygiene.
- Use disposable gloves.
- Ensure that teeth and bones are clean and sterilised before use.
- Be aware that the use of smoking machines is not always allowed.
- Avoid exercises which unreasonably test stamina or strength.
- Be aware of self-image and other emotional issues including using family trees or collecting information on weight and height.
- Be aware of ethical issues including human participants, clothing, certain foodstuffs and animals.
- Be aware of sensitivities including disabilities.

Other animals

- Ensure that animals are selected for the classroom with great care.
- Ensure that specialist advice is sought or reputable texts are consulted.
- Ensure that only reputable animal suppliers are used.
- Avoid animals that transmit diseases to humans, are difficult to keep, or cause infestation.
- Be aware that not all animals are safe to handle.
- Avoid touching animals unless it is absolutely safe to do so.
- Be aware of allergies and reactions to certain animals.
- Ensure meticulous attention to personal hygiene.

- Use disposable gloves.
- Never keep wild animals brought in by children.
- Be aware of laws governing collecting or disturbing certain rare or endangered and protected species.
- Do not keep mammals or birds in rooms where humans work regularly.
- Ensure that cages and aquariums are cleaned regularly.
- Restrict the free movement and access of animals.
- Prevent contamination of foodstuffs.
- Ensure the care, safety and well-being of animals, especially during weekends and longer breaks.
- Treat bites and stings immediately.
- Avoid working in areas with contaminated soils (e.g. by glass, faeces, fertilisers).
- Ensure that all animals collected from the wild are returned.
- Be aware of sensitivities involving animal experimentation.

Green plants

- Be aware that not all plants are safe to handle.
- Be aware that some wild flowers are protected or endangered and should not be picked at all.
- Avoid touching, tasting or eating plants unless it is absolutely safe to do so (including fruits and seeds).
- Avoid plants which sting or bear thorns.
- Be aware of allergies and reactions to certain plants.
- Avoid working in areas with contaminated soils (e.g. by glass, faeces, fertlisers).
- Ensure meticulous attention to personal hygiene.
- Use disposable gloves.

Living things in their environment

See also comments on *humans*, *other animals* and *green plants* above.

- Avoid unnecessary exposure to the sun.
- Avoid unnecessary exposure to harsh weather conditions.
- Avoid working in areas with contaminated soils (e.g. glass, faeces, fertlisers).
- Avoid touching, tasting or eating plants unless it is absolutely safe to do so (including fruits and seeds).
- Avoid touching animals unless it is absolutely safe to do so.
- Ensure sensible precautions when conducting litter surveys.
- Ensure meticulous attention to personal hygiene.
- Use disposable gloves.
- Ensure only safe sources of micro-organisms are used and are disposed of safely.

PRACTICAL TASK PRACTICAL TASK **PRACTICAL TASK** PRACTICAL TASK

Make sure that you have consulted all the sources of information provided here before you next teach science (see **Research summary, Further reading** and **References**). Where appropriate, pay particular attention to the legal requirements for keeping living things in the classroom. Demonstrate that you have considered health and safety by making a clear health and safety statement in your planning. Always **be safe!**

Materials

- Be aware of and avoid flammable and toxic materials and materials which cause irritation.
- Be aware of and ensure that only approved acids and alkalis are used.
- Avoid using very fine powders and materials which produce fine dusts when cut.
- Avoid superglues and adhesives which give off strong fumes.
- Avoid using boiling water and steam directly from kettles.
- Avoid gases other than air or the carbon dioxide in fizzy drinks.
- Burn only small amounts of materials under strict supervision.
- Avoid naked flames other than using candles in sand trays.
- Use cookers, hot plates, microwaves, fridges and freezers under strict supervision.

Figure 10.1 How many health and safety violations can you find? Cartoons likes this can be used to help children identify hazards and risks and to carry out primary science safely.

Electricity and magnetism

- Ensure that all mains appliances are thoroughly and regularly checked.
- Be aware of the dangers of using mains electricity.

- Be aware that not all batteries are safe to use in school.
- Avoid cutting batteries open.
- Ensure that loose iron filings are stored securely and only used in sealed containers.
- Be aware that small magnets could be swallowed or placed in ears and noses.
- Ensure that electromagnets do not overheat.

Forces and motion

- Ensure that fingers and toes are kept well away from heavy objects likely to fall on or roll over them when released down ramps or in free-fall.
- Ensure eye protection is worn when stretching springs and elastic bands or when twisting and bending brittle materials.
- Avoid climbing on chairs and tables when releasing 'helicopters' and other flying objects.
- Avoid reckless throwing of paper darts and gliders.
- Be aware of breathing difficulties if playing games like 'blow football'.

Light and sound

- Protect eyes at all times.
- Avoid shining bright lights into eyes.
- Avoid using mirrors and lenses with rough or sharp edges.
- Avoid foreign objects from entering eyes.
- Protect ears at all times.
- Avoid listening to loud sounds for any length of time.
- Avoid foreign objects from entering ears.

The earth and beyond

- Avoid looking directly at the sun at all times and *never* look directly at the sun through binoculars or a telescope.
- Supervise all indirect observations of the sun.
- Avoid observing the moon through binoculars or a telescope for long periods of time.
- Be aware that some models of the solar system and the earth–sun–moon system contain small parts which could be swallowed or placed in ears and noses.
- Ensure that parents are informed of homework activities which require observations of the night sky.

Using computers

- Ensure safe and comfortable working conditions at all times (select suitable benches and chairs with height, reach and posture in mind).
- Store cables and other loose wiring away from feet.
- Avoid placing food and drink near computers or other electrical appliances.
- Be aware of neck strain, eye strain and repetitive strain injuries when using computers for long periods of time.
- Avoid excessive screen glare and reflection.
- Be aware of crowding around computers.

Next time you are in school, look around for evidence of good health and safety practice. Is there a health and safety policy available? What information does it contain? Is there a central health and safety notice board? Are there any up-to-date health and safety newsletters pinned to it? Is there a nominated health and safety representative or contact for primary science? Are there any health and safety posters or displays available for or produced by children? Do health and safety feature prominently in science teaching? Is your school safe and healthy?

Off-site visits

Off-site visits involve children and teachers in travelling and working beyond school grounds. Off-site visits therefore include day trips to local parks and ponds, museums and science centres, zoos, botanical gardens and wildlife centres, and beaches. They also include residential trips to environmental and other field study centres. Off-site visits require special attention:

- **Nominated leaders should be suitably trained, qualified and experienced.**
- **Nominated leaders, together with all accompanying teachers, are ultimately responsible and accountable for everything that occurs.**
- **Only approved transportation operators should be used (e.g. minibus, coach, train, underground).**
- **Only approved locations and environmental and other field study centres should be used.**
- **A thorough risk assessment should always be carried out in advance of the trip and following a reconnaissance visit to the locations involved.**
- **Proper consultation should always take place with headteachers and, if appropriate, governing bodies.**
- **Proper consultation should always take place with parents and guardians and prior permission should always be obtained in writing.**
- **Communication between the travelling party and the school should be possible at all times (e.g. by mobile phone).**
- **All codes of conduct offered by schools, LAs and other responsible bodies should be followed rigorously.**

IN THE CLASSROOM

Mrs Evans and Mr Davies were getting ready to take their classes to the city museum for the last of several visits while teaching about humans and other animals. The museum was five miles away and the children were coached there and back by an approved operator. Leaving the school, Mr D let Mrs E know that he had counted 59 children on board. The visit passed by without incident, as usual, and Mrs E counted 59 children back onto the coach. Both teachers had been back at the school for about 15 minutes when the school secretary came running into the staff room to tell them that they'd left a child behind! But how had this happened? How it had happened was easy: Mr D had miscounted. There were, of course, sixty children present. Both teachers should have counted independently, probably twice, and cross-checked. Mrs E, thinking that all were back on board, instructed the driver to go. While counting independently and cross-checking would not have revealed the missing child, had both teachers miscounted initially, a simple check around the museum galleries would have revealed their mistake. Both teachers were at fault. Fortunately for them, the child was 'retrieved' safely, praised for his outstanding interest in science, and the matter passed without further incident. Some schools assign children to specific seats and keep a seating plan readily available on such trips. This is a much better strategy than counting.

First-aid and administration of medication

No teacher is obliged to become a first-aider or an appointed first-aider within a school. All teachers should, however, know who these people are, where they can be found when needed, and where the nearest first-aid box is. All teachers should be familiar with school rules and procedures for dealing with and reporting accidents requiring first-aid. Only appointed first-aiders are usually responsible for:

- maintaining and updating first-aid boxes;
- taking charge of emergency situations;
- administering emergency first-aid where they have been trained and feel confident and competent to do so.

At the time of a serious accident, one which requires prompt and immediate action, teachers may be required to deal with the emergency while waiting for a first-aider or other help to arrive. Serious accidents might include:

- burns and scalds;
- cuts and bleeding;
- bites and scratches;
- spillages of chemicals onto skin;
- splashes of chemicals into eyes;
- ingestion of certain food substances, chemicals and poisons;
- choking and other breathing difficulties;
- electric shock and electrocution;
- loss of consciousness.

The St John Ambulance publication *Emergency Aid in Schools* (2006) does provide help and St John Ambulance will advise on suitable courses of first-aid training. Just as no teacher is obliged to become a first-aider or an appointed first-aider within a school, no teacher is obliged to administer medicines or to supervise children taking them, particularly if the timing of administration is crucial to a child's health or where medical and technical knowledge is required. All teachers should, however, know which of their children require medication to be administered during the school day, the properly qualified, trained and appointed individuals within the school responsible for undertaking such tasks, and the school's procedures for dealing with medical emergencies. All teachers should be familiar with school rules and regulations for receiving, handling and storing medicines. Any of the teachers' unions will provide clear guidance on all of these issues.

IN THE CLASSROOM

Chris had been swinging backwards and forwards on his chair all morning. His teacher, working with a group investigating forces at another table, had told him twice already to stop and what might happen if he didn't. Eventually Chris did fall over. In fact, he disappeared from view with a bit of a thud! 'Are you going to lie there all day Chris, or are you going to join the rest of us and do some work?' his teacher called out. 'He's bleeding sir!' came a shout from the girl sitting next to him. What would you have done? Fortunately, Chris's teacher knew exactly what to do. Noting the large cut above Chris's eye, and the amount of bleeding involved (Chris had hit his head on the edge of the desk as he went down), the class were settled quickly into their seats. Two children were sent to get the deputy headteacher immediately. After hastily putting on the protective gloves kept in the teacher's desk, direct pressure was applied to Chris's wound to help stop the bleeding. Once the deputy headteacher arrived and took over, Chris's teacher left the room to arrange for Chris to visit the local health centre and for Chris's parents to be informed. The school caretaker was called in to deal with the blood on the classroom floor. The whole incident was dealt with in minutes. Chris returned to school later that day. The incident was used to illustrate how easily accidents happen without due care and attention and to praise the children for their calm and appropriate behaviour.

Teaching about health and safety

Teaching about health and safety in primary science should be looked upon as a routine part of teaching science as a whole. Useful teaching strategies include:

- **effective questioning (e.g. 'What do you think will happen if . . . ?', 'Who can tell me . . . ?', 'Why do you think . . . ?');**
- **instruction, demonstration and explanation (e.g. safe ways to proceed, what to do and not to do and why);**
- **display (e.g. health and safety symbols, children's posters and formal science reports, written and pictorial reminders);**
- **classroom rules and procedures (e.g. noise levels, movement around the classroom, appropriate behaviour, accident and emergency drills);**
- **example (e.g. practise what you preach).**

Children's knowledge and understanding of the importance of health and safety should progress throughout the primary years. By the end of Key Stage 1, children should be able to recognise that there are hazards and dangers associated with certain aspects of primary science (scientific enquiry, life processes and living things, materials and their properties and physical processes) and, with help from their teachers, begin to identify and assess those hazards and dangers for themselves. They should also be increasingly aware of how to care for and look after each other and other living things. By the end of Key Stage 2, children should be able to routinely recognise hazards and dangers associated with certain aspects of primary science and to identify and assess those hazards and dangers for themselves. They should be encouraged and able to apply their existing knowledge and understanding of health and safety to new situations and respond accordingly.

Figure 10. 2 Safety signs for classroom use. Children could explore designing their own and choosing suitable colour combinations.

A SUMMARY OF **KEY POINTS**

> Primary schools are relatively safe places and reported accidents or incidents as a result of primary science activity are rare.

> Risk assessment and risk management can help to avoid preventable injury.

> Teachers, including trainees and NQTs, should be familiar with codes of conduct for health and safety in primary science, including those for off-site visits, for reporting accidents or incidents requiring first-aid, and for dealing with other medical emergencies.

> On matters of health and safety there is no substitute for proper training, qualifications and experience.

> Teaching about health and safety in primary science should be looked upon as a routine part of teaching science as a whole.

Moving on

As you make the transition from your course of initial teaching training into your induction period and NQT year you should continue to be vigilant with respect to all aspects of health and safety in everything you do (and not just in science). In order to do this effectively, and to continue to develop professionally, approach your induction tutor or mentor and head teacher to discuss school [policy and arrange to discuss health and safety in science with your science coordinator. It is important that you do not find yourself working in isolation. This is now unnecessary mistakes happen. Don't let them happen to you. Health and safety issues at all levels in your school will crop up fairly regularly. Observe, listen, learn and, when you're more confident, contribute.

FURTHER READING   FURTHER READING   **FURTHER READING**

CLEAPSS Guides: *PS22 Health and Safety in Primary Science and Technology* (11/98); L224 *Model Health and Safety Policy in Primary Science* (12/98); L216p *Inspecting Safety in Science – a Guide for Ofsted Inspectors in Primary Schools* (9/96). Excellent sources of relevant material discussing essential aspects of health and safety and providing guidance on risk assessment. Other specific health and safety titles available on request.

Wray, J. (ed.) (1994) *Safety in Science for Primary Schools: an Inset Pack for Use by Science*

Co-ordinators, Head Teachers, Advisory Teachers and Teacher Trainers. Hatfield: Association for Science Education. An excellent source of relevant material containing practical examples and useful advice on many common health and safety issues associated with primary science.

REFERENCES REFERENCES **REFERENCES** REFERENCES REFERENCES

Abbott, C. (ed.) (2001) *Be Safe! Some Aspects of Safety in School Science and Technology for Key Stages 1 and 2*. Hatfield: Association for Science Education.
St John Ambulance (2006) *Emergency Aid in Schools*. London: Order of St John.

Excellent sources of relevant materials discussing essential aspects of health and safety can be found via the following websites:

The Association for Science Education: *http://www.ase.org.uk.*

The Department for Education and Skills: *http://www.dfes.gov.uk.*

The School Science Service: *http://www.cleapss.org.uk.*

The Scottish Schools Equipment Research Centre: *http://www.sserc.org.uk.*

Glossary

analogy A description or physical representation of something which behaves in a similar way to a science concept which enables the learner to gain a better understanding of the concept, e.g. the analogy of current flow in a circuit to the flow of water in pipes.

buffer box A box which has sensors plugged into it. In turn the buffer box is plugged into the computer.

CD-ROM A disc which contains information or programs.

closed question A question to which the range of answers is limited – often to a single, correct answer.

concept mapping A diagram in which science concepts or ideas, often in text form, are linked to show their relationships. Concept maps can be used to reveal a learner's understanding within a wide conceptual area such as 'light'.

conceptual understanding An understanding of scientific ideas, for example force.

criterion referenced Related to specific behaviour or benchmarks.

database A program which collates data.

datalogger The kit required to sense the environment (e.g. temperature, sound or light) which includes a buffer box, sensor and software.

diagnostic Assessment through which difficulties can be recognised in order to inform the next teaching step. This is distinct from formative assessment in that diagnostic assessment is usually done by an expert in a particular field (e.g. profound learning difficulties) with the process taking considerable time.

differentiation Provision made by the teacher to enable children of different ability to learn effectively.

elicitation Techniques used to find out what children know and understand about a scientific idea or concept.

evaluative Assessment which is planned to evaluate the success of some teaching. This form of assessment could be used, for instance, to check whether one form of teaching reading is more effective than another.

evidence Information gathered to support or disprove an idea.

Excel A proprietary spreadsheet program for a PC.

formal Planned for and sometimes recorded.

formative Assessment to recognise the child's achievements and difficulties to inform the next teaching step. This is distinct from diagnostic testing in that teachers normally carry out formative assessment during ordinary teaching activities.

generalisation A statement which describes a series of observations which have something in common, e.g. most metals conduct electricity well.

Google One of many search engines.

hypothesis An explanation that leads to a prediction which can be tested. It draws upon some scientific knowledge. A prediction may be based on previous experience or reasoned expectations without drawing upon scientific knowledge or being phrased in a way that can be tested.

illustrative activities Practical activities in which children are guided towards understanding a particular scientific idea.

informal assessment Not planned for and generally unrecorded.

internet A system of computers linked by telephone lines.

iterative Comparing with child's previous performance.

keys Systematic ways of identifying animals or plants. The simplest binomial keys have questions to which the answer is either yes or no, so that answering the questions in turn leads to the correct name for whatever has to be identified. For example, a key for identifying trees by their leaves might ask, 'Is the leaf made up of smaller leaves?' If the answer is 'no' that leads to a further question which applies to simple leaves, then to another and so on until it is identified. Biological keys are the commonest but they can be used to identify materials. Questions have to be carefully worded. Children can understand keys better if they first make their own for a few objects and then learn to use published keys with increasing sophistication. Computers are useful for making their own and for using existing keys on software.

learning objectives A description of the learning the teacher expects the children to achieve.

learning outcomes A description of the learning the children are expected to demonstrate in order to show success in the learning objectives.

lesson evaluation A reflective and critical account of a teaching unit which highlights both the children's and the teachers' responses and sets out targets for the future.

lesson pace The rate at which the various learning experiences change within a single lesson.

lesson structure The form that a lesson takes in terms of timing and features such as lesson introduction, development and conclusion.

long-term planning An overview of the learning programmes for a whole school over the period of a complete year – often described as a scheme of work.

medium-term planning A broad plan of the learning programme for typically a half term or whole term – often described as a topic plan. Some schemes of work include detailed medium-term planning.

model Something which represents and behaves similarly to a phenomenon in the real world, e.g. a picture of the molecules in a solid, liquid or gas.

multimedia A computer program which uses text, sound and images.

norm referenced Children measured against others.

open question A question to which there is a wide range of acceptable answers.

practical activity A learning situation in which children have some hands-on experience using physical equipment.

predict Make an informed statement about something which will happen in the future.

procedural understanding An understanding of the ways in which science works, the processes and methods used in science. This involves bringing together the skills that will be needed to carry out an investigation with an understanding of the procedures such as designing appropriate investigations, deciding what measurements to take, how to present and interpret data, whether they are valid.

progression Provision which will enable a child to move forward in understanding within a subject.

reliability The degree of trust we should place in the data – i.e. whether the experiment is likely to yield similar results if repeated.

restructuring The reforming of science concepts as a result of a learning experience.

scheme of work See long-term and medium-term plans.

science The study of how and why everything in the universe behaves the way it does.

science concept A 'big idea' in science such as force or the particle theory of matter.

science enquiry A learning experience in which the child takes some responsibility for planning, executing and reflecting on an investigation of a science phenomenon.

scientific community Scientists around the world who communicate with each other, constructively criticise each other's findings and share some common beliefs about science concepts.

scientific skills A range of abilities which enable people to behave scientifically.

scientific theory A description made to explain a collection of scientific observations which can then be subjected to scrutiny by the scientific community and matched against a range of evidence which might support or disprove it.

search engine A site on the Internet which searches for information which you request.

secondary sources Information which is gained, not through first-hand experience but through the use of sources such as books, ICT or discussions with others.

short-term planning Lesson planning.

SI units Standard international units of measurement and abbreviations are used in science, for example newtons (N) are the unit for measuring forces.

spreadsheet A program which allows data to be entered into a table. The data can then be used in calculations or the production of graphs.

standardised Related to a set of generally accepted criteria.

summative Where assessment is recorded systematically with the aim of establishing markers showing children's achievement. This is usually done at the end of a key stage or at the end of year.

teacher exposition The provision of information which is provided directly by the teacher orally, often within the introduction to a lesson.

teaching objectives The objectives which a teacher has for a learning programme such as a single lesson. These are often set out in terms of the intended learning objectives for the children.

technology The application of scientific ideas, as well as those from other disciplines, in order to solve a human problem or need.

template A document created using either a spreadsheet or word processor which is saved as a template (on PCs) or stationery (Macs). If opened and altered the changed version is saved, leaving the original template unaltered.

validity Whether an investigation answers the question. In an experiment, procedures such as controlling variables are used so the data is more likely to be valid.

variables: *Continuous* when they can have any value on a scale (for example, temperature or length).

Discrete when they can only have whole number values (for example, the number of layers of tissue paper needed to stop light shining through).

Categoric when we just assign things to a particular category (for example, boys and girls; eye colours).

variation between repeated measurements of the same thing may derive from unexpected differences in what is being investigated or from errors. Because it is difficult to do exactly the same on every test we get random experimental error which may make our measurement larger or smaller. We can attempt to reduce this by taking an average of several measurements. But averaging will not compensate for a systematic error that always affects our measurement in the same direction.

webcam A camera connected up to the net directly and for long periods allowing distant observers to see what is happening.

Index

Achieving QTS

The Achieving QTS series continues to grow with nearly 50 titles in 8 separate strands. Our titles address issues of teaching and learning across both primary and secondary phases in a highly practical and accessible manner, making each title an invaluable resource for trainee teachers.

We've updated and improved 13 of our bestselling titles in line with the new Standards for QTS (September 2007). These titles are highlighted with a * in the list below.

Assessment for Learning and Teaching in Primary Schools
Mary Briggs, Angela Woodfield, Cynthia Martin and Peter Swatton
£15   176 pages   ISBN: 978 1 903300 74 9

Assessment for Learning and Teaching in Secondary Schools
Martin Fautley and Jonathan Savage
£16   160 pages   ISBN: 978 1 84445 107 4

***Learning and Teaching in Secondary Schools (third edition)**
Viv Ellis
£16   192 pages   ISBN: 978 1 84445 096 1

Learning and Teaching Using ICT in Secondary Schools
John Woollard
£17.50   192 pages   ISBN: 978 1 84445 078 7

Passing the ICT Skills Test (second edition)
Clive Ferrigan
£8   80 pages   ISBN: 978 1 84445 028 2

Passing the Literacy Skills Test
Jim Johnson
£8   80 pages   ISBN: 978 1 903300 12 1

Passing the Numeracy Skills Test (third edition)
Mark Patmore,
£8   64 pages   ISBN: 978 1 903300 94 7

***Primary English: Audit and Test (third edition)**
Doreen Challen
£9   64 pages   ISBN: 978 1 84445 110 4

***Primary English: Knowledge and Understanding (third edition)**
Jane Medwell, George Moore, David Wray and Vivienne Griffiths
£16   240 pages   ISBN: 978 1 84445 093 0

***Primary English: Teaching Theory and Practice (third edition)**
Jane Medwell, David Wray, Hilary Minns, Vivienne Griffiths and Liz Coates
£16   208 pages   ISBN: 978 1 84445 092 3

***Primary ICT: Knowledge, Understanding and Practice (third edition)**
Jonathan Allen, John Potter, Jane Sharp and Keith Turvey
£16   256 pages   ISBN: 978 1 84445 094 7

***Primary Mathematics: Audit and Test (third edition)**
Claire Mooney and Mike Fletcher
£9   52 pages   ISBN: 978 1 84445 111 1

*Primary Mathematics: Knowledge and Understanding (third edition)
Claire Mooney, Lindsey Ferrie, Sue Fox, Alice Hansen and Reg Wrathmell
£16   176 pages   ISBN: 978 1 84445 053 4

*Primary Mathematics: Teaching Theory and Practice (third edition)
Claire Mooney, Mary Briggs, Mike Fletcher, Alice Hansen and Judith McCullouch
£16   192 pages   ISBN: 978 1 84445 099 2

*Primary Science: Audit and Test (third edition)
John Sharp and Jenny Byrne
£9   80 pages   ISBN: 978 1 84445 109 8

*Primary Science: Knowledge and Understanding (third edition)
Graham Peacock, John Sharp, Rob Johnsey and Debbie Wright
£16   240 pages   ISBN: 978 1 84445 098 5

*Primary Science: Teaching Theory and Practice (third edition)
Rob Johnsey, John Sharp, Graham Peacock, Shirley Simon and Robin Smith
£16   144 pages   ISBN: 978 1 84445 097 8

*Professional Studies: Primary and Early Years (third edition)
Kate Jacques and Rob Hyland
£16   256 pages   ISBN: 978 1 84445 095 4

Teaching Arts in Primary Schools
Raywen Ford, Stephanie Penny, Lawry Price and Susan Young
£15   192 pages   ISBN: 978 1 903300 35 0

Teaching Design and Technology at Key Stages 1 and 2
Gill Hope
£17   224 pages   ISBN: 978 1 84445 056 5

Teaching Foundation Stage
Iris Keating
£15   200 pages   ISBN: 978 1 903300 33 6

Teaching Humanities in Primary Schools
Editor: Pat Hoodless
£15   192 pages   ISBN: 978 1 903300 36 7

Teaching Religious Education: Primary and Early Years
Elaine McCreery, Sandra Palmer and Veronica Voiels
£16   176 pages   ISBN: 978 1 84445 108 1

Achieving QTS Cross-Curricular Strand

Children's Spiritual, Moral, Social and Cultural Development
Tony Eaude
£14   128 pages   ISBN: 978 1 84445 048 0

Creativity in Primary Education
Anthony Wilson
£15   224 pages   ISBN: 978 1 84445 013 8

Creativity in Secondary Education
Jonathan Savage, Martin Fautley
£16   144 pages   ISBN: 978 1 84445 073 2

Teaching Citizenship in Primary Schools
Editor: Hilary Claire
£15   192 pages   ISBN: 978 1 84445 010 7

Teaching Literacy Across the Primary Curriculum
David Wray
£14   144 pages   ISBN: 978 1 84445 008 4

Achieving QTS Extending Knowledge in Practice

Primary English: Extending Knowledge in Practice
Jane Medwell and David Wray
£16   160 pages   ISBN: 978 1 84445 104 3

Primary ICT: Extending Knowledge in Practice
John Duffty
£16   176 pages   ISBN: 978 1 84445 055 8

Primary Mathematics: Extending Knowledge in Practice
Alice Hansen
£16   176 pages   ISBN: 978 1 84445 054 1

Primary Science: Extending Knowledge in Practice
Judith Roden, Hellen Ward and Hugh Ritchie
£16   160 pages   ISBN: 978 1 84445 106 7

Achieving QTS Practical Handbooks

Learning and Teaching with Interactive Whiteboards: Primary and Early Years
David Barber, Linda Cooper, Graham Meeson
£14   128 pages   ISBN: 978 1 84445 081 7

Learning and Teaching with Virtual Learning Environments
Helena Gillespie, Helen Boulton, Alison Hramiak and Richard Williamson
£14   144 pages   ISBN: 978 1 84445 076 3

***Successful Teaching Placement: Primary and Early Years (second edition)**
Jane Medwell
£12   160 pages   ISBN: 978 1 84445 091 6

Using Resources to Support Mathematical Thinking: Primary and Early Years
Doreen Drews and Alice Hansen
£15   160 pages   ISBN: 978 1 84445 057 2

Achieving QTS Reflective Readers

Primary English Reflective Reader
Andrew Lambirth
£14   128 pages   ISBN: 978 1 84445 035 0

Primary Mathematics Reflective Reader
Louise O'Sullivan, Andrew Harris, Gina Donaldson, Gill Bottle, Margaret Sangster and
Jon Wild
£14   120 pages   ISBN: 978 1 84445 036 7

Primary Professional Studies Reflective Reader
Sue Kendall-Seater
£15   192 pages   ISBN: 978 1 84445 033 6

Primary Science Reflective Reader
Judith Roden
£14   128 pages   ISBN: 978 1 84445 037 4

Primary Special Educational Needs Reflective Reader
Sue Soan
£14   136 pages   ISBN: 978 1 84445 038 1

Secondary Professional Studies Reflective Reader
Simon Hoult
£14   192 pages   ISBN: 978 1 84445 034 3

Secondary Science Reflective Reader
Gren Ireson and John Twidle
£16   128 pages   ISBN: 978 1 84445 065 7

To order please phone our order line 0845 230 9000 or send an official order or cheque to BEBC, Albion Close, Parkstone, Poole, BH12 3LL
Order online at www.learningmatters.co.uk